Cases, (& Theories

MW00893312

Media Law and Ethics
Study Guide No. 4.1

Published By

George Padgett

January 2020

THIRD ACT
BOOKS

Burlington, North Carolina

Other Books Published by the Author:

Along the Way: Stories from An Ordinary Life
Random Acts: An Eli Hurlbert Mystery
Just the Facts: Murder on the McKinley
University Campus
New Directions in Diversity (Non-fiction)

Author's Note

The material in this book is produced entirely by the author who takes full responsibility for its content. It includes summaries of legal cases related to the study of media law, a brief catalog of legal and First Amendment terms, concepts and theories, media organization ethics codes, and materials that may be helpful in preparing class assignments and studying for exams. It also includes a complete copy of the United States Constitution and the Amendments. It is a work in progress and the author appreciates comments, including corrections and suggestions for improvement. Please feel free to send any communications to padgettg@elon.edu.

Contents

Introduction

Given the complexity of the American legal system, media law can be a daunting topic for many undergraduate students with a full slate of classes and extracurricular activities. Add to that a dose of ethical decision-making formulas, philosophical theories, and esoteric terms and the challenge becomes even greater.

Major publishers don't help the situation with their 500-page plus textbooks filled with page after gray page of legal terms, state and federal acts, and rulings from state, federal and appeals courts. When they finally do get to the U.S. Supreme Court decisions, the significance is buried in an abundance of gibberish, largely and unnecessarily confusing to anyone without a law degree.

Therefore, *Cases, Concepts & Theories: Media Law and Ethics Study Guide*. It is not intended to be a textbook, but rather a launching point for a semester-long study of legal topics including an introduction to the U.S. Supreme Court and the American legal system, libel, invasion of privacy, access to public records, copyright, indecency and obscenity, broadcast regulation, and commercial speech. For those who still want a traditional text, there are a number of good ones on the market. Simply go to Amazon.com, type in "media law textbook" and your dreams will be immediately realized.

On the other hand, if you just want the basics needed to conquer an undergraduate level course in media law and ethics, this may be the solution. The meat of this guide is an accumulation of relevant court cases with brief summaries explaining in simple terms the decisions and their significance to students of media law and professional media and communications practitioners. The second most important part of this study guide is an A to Z collection of concepts, theories, definitions, and assorted facts related to media law and ethics topics.

Also included are a list of helpful law and ethics-related websites, copies of ethics codes from major professional media organizations, hypotheticals to challenge your thinking, an outline to use when studying for exams, a sample syllabus, and a complete copy of the U.S. Constitution and its amendments.

Two additional notes: First, the material included in this guide is largely from legal and governmental sources that are not protected by copyright and thus may be used by anyone; and from my own personal experiences as a journalist and as a student and professor of media law and ethics. I am solely responsible for the contents of this guide. I alone determined what materials would be included, the arrangement of materials and the design. Where interpretation is involved, I am solely responsible for that interpretation.

Second and finally, these materials are organized specifically for the author's section or sections of *COMM 400 Media Law and Ethics* at Elon University. However, I gladly offer anyone who finds it useful permission to adapt any of these materials for their own educational purposes. The only restriction I ask is that you not use my work for commercial gain and that you give the author credit for any materials repurposed in a different format.

Please feel free to contact me with questions or comments at padgettg@elon.edu.

Case Summaries

Following in alphabetical order are summaries of media law cases relevant to most students in courses in media or mass communications law. Topics range from libel and privacy to obscenity, broadcast indecency and commercial speech. A final section addresses cases involving freedom of religion, both the establishment and the free exercise clauses.

The entries are not intended to provide comprehensive coverage of any case, but rather to focus on why the case is important to the study of media law and what important precedent it does or does not set. Additional information can be obtained by searching for the full case at one of the following excellent online sources: findlaw.com, oyez.org, or justia.com.

Finally, most of the cases included in this section are cases that have been decided by the United States Supreme Court. Some, like those related to the censorship of public school student posts on blogs and social media sites such as Facebook, are Circuit or Appeals Court decisions.

Issues in Free Expression

Abrams v. U.S., 1919 – upheld the Espionage Act conviction of four radicals who protested President Woodrow Wilson's decision to send troops into Russia following the Bolshevik Revolution. They had thrown leaflets from the tops of buildings in NYC urging a general strike in protest. In his dissent, Holmes added to his clear and present danger test that the danger of substantive evil must be "imminent and forthwith."

Barber v. Dearborn Public Schools, 2003 – Federal court ruled that a Michigan student had the right to wear a T-shirt with a picture of President George W. Bush's face and the caption "International Terrorist" on school grounds, reaffirming Tinker v. Des Moines and students' free speech rights.

Bell v. Itawamba County School Board, 2016 – USSC denied certiorari, thus upholding a decision of the 5th Circuit Court of Appeals that the county school board had properly suspended a student for inappropriate posts on Facebook and YouTube. The case involved 18-year-old Taylor Bell who had posted violent rap lyrics he had written claiming that two of the school's coaches were sexually harassing female students. In ruling against Bell, the 5th Circuit noted that the rap song could cause "substantial disruption" in the school and therefore was not protected by the First Amendment. <u>The decision is the latest in a series of inconsistent rulings addressing the issue of student rights re off campus speech.</u>

Bethel School District v. Fraser, 1986 – Court ruled that schools could limit/sanction lewd, vulgar, offensive remarks by a student in public assembly. Considered one of the three most significant school rulings . . . Tinker, Kuhlmeier, Fraser. If you add in the recent Morse case, in spite of the ruling in Tinker, courts have been stingy with First Amendment rights when public school students are involved.

Board of Education v. Pico, 1982 - ruled that school officials could not remove books from the library because they disagreed with the ideas in the books. However, the court determined that officials could remove the books if they were "pervasively vulgar" or educationally unsuitable.

Brandenburg v. Ohio, 1969 – law must distinguish between advocacy of ideas, and the incitement to unlawful conduct. (Targeted speech much be directed at inciting or producing imminent lawless action and be likely to produce or incite such action.)

The Brandenburg Incitement Test
1. Does the expression advocate the use of illegal force or violence?
2. Is it directed toward actually inciting such illegal conduct?
3. Would the advised conduct be imminent, or immediate?
4. Is the expression likely to produce the illegal conduct?

Bridges v. California, 1941 - Harry Bridges, the leader of a longshoreman's union, sent a telegram to the Secretary of Labor, regarding a case pending that was in the Superior Court of Los Angeles County. Bridges implied that he would have his union go on strike if the Superior Court ruled unfavorably. A copy of the telegram was distributed to various West Coast Newspapers. The Superior Court found Bridges in contempt of court and fined him. Similarly, the Los Angeles Times was also found in contempt of court and fined for publishing several editorials regarding a case pending in the Superior Court. Bridges and the Times challenged their punishments separately in the Superior Court. The Superior Court upheld their fines, and both appealed separately to the Supreme Court of California. The California Supreme Court affirmed the Superior Court. Bridges and the Times appealed separately to the Supreme Court, where the cases were consolidated. In a 5-4 decision, the Court reversed the Supreme Court of California and found the fines for contempt unconstitutional.

Burstyn v. Wilson, 1952 – Ruled invalid provisions of the New York Education Law, which forbid the commercial showing of any motion picture film without a license and authorized denial of a license on a censor's conclusion that a film is "sacrilegious." Ruling declared expression by means of motion pictures is included within the free speech and free press guaranty of the First and Fourteenth Amendments and noted that motion pictures are a significant medium for the communication of ideas. . . not lessened by the fact that they are designed to entertain as well as to inform.

Chaplinsky v. New Hampshire, 1942 – defined fighting words as those which by their very utterance inflict injury or tend to incite an immediate breach of peace. In this case, a JW called a town marshal a G-damned racketeer and fascist, violating a state law forbidding derisive or abusive language. The decision stated: "It has been well observed that such utterances are no essential part of any exposition of ideas, and are of such slight social value as a step to truth that any benefit may be derived from them is clearly outweighed by the social interest in order and morality."

City of Houston v. Hill, 1987 – Court struck down the conviction of an individual for making offensive comments to a police officer. "The freedom of individuals verbally to oppose or challenge police action without thereby risking arrest is one of the principal characteristics by which we distinguish a free nation from a police state," Brennan wrote.

Cohen v. California, 1971– Writing that "one man's vulgarity is another's lyric," Justice John Harlan's opinion in this important 5-4 decision holds that the First Amendment protects even language that some find to be vulgar or offensive. The case involves 19-year-old Paul Cohen who wore a jacket emblazoned with "Fuck the Draft. Stop the War" in protest of the Vietnam War. He was initially charged under a California statute, which prohibits "maliciously and willfully disturb[ing] the peace and quiet of any neighborhood or person [by] offensive conduct." The court found that the language was not obscene, was not directed at anyone in particular and did not constitute fighting words.

Doninger v. Niehoff, 2008 – A federal appeals court ruled that a high school was within its rights to punish a student for writing critical comments about school administrators on the Internet. The 2nd U.S. Circuit Court of Appeals said Lewis Mills High School in Burlington, Conn., has a responsibility like any school to teach students the boundaries of socially appropriate behavior. "Vulgar or offensive speech — speech that an adult making a political point might have a constitutional right to employ — may legitimately give rise to disciplinary action by a school," the unanimous three-judge panel ruled in. She was disqualified from running for senior class secretary. Doninger was disciplined after she used derogatory language to describe the administrators in a blog entry she made outside of school in April 2007."We have determined . . . that a student may be disciplined for expressive conduct, even conduct occurring off school grounds, when this conduct 'would foreseeably create a risk of substantial disruption within the school environment.'

Dennis v. U.S., 1951 – In a 6-to-2 decision, the Court upheld the convictions of the Communist Party leaders and found that the Smith Act did not "inherently" violate the First Amendment. In the plurality opinion, the Court held that there was a distinction between the mere teaching of communist philosophies and active advocacy of those ideas. Such advocacy created a "clear and present danger" that threatened the government.

Elonis v. United States, 2015 – ruled that comments, including graphically violent rap lyrics and imagery, that Elonis directed at his estranged wife, coworkers and law enforcement officials on Facebook did not constitute a "true threat," in that the communications did not include a subjective intent to threaten.

Erie v. Pap's A.M., 2000 – ruled that an ordinance banning public nudity (nude dancing) was not in violation of the free speech rights of the owner of Kandyland, a bar/nightclub in Erie, Pa., thus upholding a local ordinance that made it illegal to "knowingly or intentionally appear in public in a state of nudity." In reasoning that the ordinance was content neutral, the Court applied the O'Brien test and the intermediate scrutiny guideline, ruling that (1) while some level of expression may be involved in nude dancing, the state of nudity itself is not inherently an expression (the same expression, for example, could be made by a dancer with even minimal clothing); (2) there was substantial government interest in controlling the negative secondary effects of a nude dancing establishment (drugs and prostitution); and (3) the suppression was not greater than necessary to achieve that effect. In a 1991 decision (Barnes v. Glen Theatre, Inc.), the Court had determined that requiring dancers to wear G-strings and pasties was not a restriction on the First Amendment.

Evans v. Bayer, 2010 – Katherine Evans created an off-campus Facebook account in which she complained about "the worst teacher I've ever met." The public high school's principal chose to punish her by removing her from AP classes at the school and by suspending her for three days. She filed suit and a federal district court ruled that since her speech was neither disruptive (Tinker) or vulgar (Bethel) the principal could not punish her. The case is important in that it signifies a movement toward protecting student speech while off campus.

Gitlow v. New York, 1925 – Extends First Amendment protection by interpreting 14th Amendment as preventing abridgement of speech or press by state governments . . . extended to include local and regional as well.

Gooding v. Wilson, 1972 – Court ruled that fighting words laws must be restricted to words that have a direct tendency to cause acts of violence by the person to whom the remarks are made. Case struck down a Georgia state law, which provided that, "Any person who shall, without provocation, use to or of another, and in his presence . . . opprobrious words or abusive language, tending to cause a breach of the peace . . . shall be guilty of a misdemeanor."

Grosjean v. American Press Co., 1936 – Invalidated a tax on newspapers that had been imposed by Louisiana governor Huey Long as a means of punishing (and ultimately suppressing) newspapers, which were critical of him. Justice George Sutherland wrote that the people "are entitled to full information in respect of the doings or misdoings of their government; informed public opinion is the most potent of all restraints upon misgovernment."

Hazelwood v. Kuhlmeier, 1988 – In a 5-3 decision, the Supreme Court ruled that when a high school principal removed articles on teenage pregnancy and the impact of divorce on children, he was exercising reasonable censorship of a school sponsored newspaper, published as a part of a class. Or: Administrators of public high schools have the right to censor school-sponsored papers, particularly those published as a part of a class. Note distinction between this case and Tinker. Tinker involved personal expression. Hazelwood involved expression as part of school curriculum.

Houston v. Hill, 1987 – ruled as an unconstitutional infringement of free speech a Houston ordinance which made it "unlawful for any person to assault, strike or in any manner oppose, molest, abuse or interrupt any policeman in the execution of his duty, or any person summoned to aid in making an arrest." Hill had simply shouted (Why don't you pick on somebody your own size.) at a police officer in an attempt to interrupt him while he was arresting a friend.

Hosty v. Carter, 2005 (appellate court ruling) – ruled that a university could require prior review and approval of the contents of a student newspaper. . . refuting the argument of a difference between high school and university; and declaring he newspaper a non-public forum. Applies to school in the three states covered by the Seventh Circuit Court of Appeals: Illinois, Indiana, and Wisconsin. As a result of the decision, SPJ and SPLC have instituted a campaign urging university administrators to declare their student newspapers as public forums . . . free from censorship and advance approval of content.

Janus v. American Federation of State, County, and Municipal Employees, Council 31, 2018 – Non-union public employees may not be charged a union fee to help pay the costs of the union negotiating for a contract that applies to all employees. Overturns 1977 decision, *Abood v. Detroit Board of Education*.

J.S. v. Blue Mountain School District, 2011 – 3rd U.S. Court of Appeals ruled that a student, J.S., could not be punished at school for a MySpace parody of her school principal, created off school grounds. Ruled that it was not enough to create a significant disruption at school. Appealed to USSC. Cert denied in January 2012.

Kara Kowalski v. Berkely County Schools, 2011 – 4th U.S. Court of Appeals upheld school's right to suspend student Kowalski for creating a web page suggesting that another student had a STD and inviting other students to comment. Appealed to USSC. Cert denied in January 2012

Kincaid v. Gibson, 2001 – Federal court ruled that Kentucky State University officials had violated the First Amendment when they confiscated the student yearbook because of the book's content and quality. The decision here points to the tendency of courts to treat students at the university level more as they would adults in a professional media world.

Landmark Communications v. Virginia, 1978 – held that a Virginia newspaper that accurately reported on a pending investigation of a state judge could not be prosecuted under a state law prohibiting anyone from divulging information about such investigations. According to the Court, the state's interest in protecting the reputation of judges was insufficient to justify the punishment of accurately reported information.

Layshock v. Hermitage School District, 2008 – U.S. district court ruled that a student's First Amendment rights were violated when his principal suspended him for content on a personal MySpace page mocking the principal. The school claims that the MySpace page was subject to school disciplinary authority, even though the page was created at a private home outside of school time, and did not threaten violence or otherwise encourage any disturbance at the school. The court found that "[t]he mere fact that the Internet may be accessed at school does not authorize school officials to become censors of the World Wide Web. Public schools are vital institutions, but their reach is not unlimited."

Lewis v. City of New Orleans, 1974 – ruled unconstitutionally overbroad a New Orleans ordinance which applied fighting words restrictions to the use of vulgar language ("you god dam mother fucking police") in reference to a police officer while performing his/her duties. Does not overrule Chaplinsky or Gooding in regards to fighting words, simply states that they do not apply.

Lovell v. Griffin, 1938 – JW arrested for distributing pamphlets in violation of city ordinances. SC ruled that the ordinance was a violation of the First Amendment. 1. Included pamphlets under First Amendment protection. 2. Protects distribution of written materials.

Marbury v. Madison, 1803 – established the concept of judicial review in the United States, setting the precedent that the U.S. Supreme Court can determine actions of the executive and legislative branches invalid based on constitutionality.

Masterpiece Cakeshop v. Colorado Civil Rights Commission, 2018 – involving the public accommodations provision of the Colorado Anti-Discrimination Act. The case stems from a 2012 conflict between Charles Craig and David Mullins and the Masterpiece Cakeshop in Lakeland, Colorado. When Craig and Mullins requested Masterpiece owner Jack Phillips design a cake for their same-sex wedding, Phillips refused on religious grounds. The baker argued that to do so would violate his religious freedom under the First Amendment's exercise clause, as well as his right to free speech (not to speak) by forcing him to create a wedding cake design. Prior to arrival at the Supreme Court, the couple received the support of the Colorado Administrative Law judge, the Colorado Civil Rights Commission, and the Colorado Court of Appeals. USSC ruled that the Civil Rights Commission conduct in evaluating the Cakeshop owner's reasons constituted a violation of the free exercise clause. In ruling for the baker, the Court also noted that at the time Phillips had refused the request from the gay couple, *Obergefell v. Hodges* (the case making same-sex marriage the law of the land) had not been decided. The issue of compelled speech was not addressed by a majority of the Court.

Minnesota Voters Alliance v. Mansky, 2018 – Ruled that a Minnesota law barring the wearing of any/all "political" (not defined by the ordinance) attire at a polling place was overbroad and thus a violation of the free speech clause of the First Amendment.

McCullen v. Coakley, 2014 – unanimously ruled that a Massachusetts law banning speech within 35 feet of any entrance to abortion clinics was a violation of the First Amendment. Said that because it allowed certain kinds of speech (clinic employees) and denied others (abortion protesters) it was not content neutral and did not meet the compelling state interest standard of strict scrutiny.

Morse v. Frederick, 2007 – SC ruled that school officials can prohibit students from displaying messages that promote illegal drug use. ["Bong Hits 4-Jesus"] Chief Justice John Roberts's majority opinion held that although students do have some right to political speech even while in school, this right does not extend to pro-drug messages that may undermine the school's important mission to discourage drug use.

National Institute of Family and Life Advocates v. Becerra, 2018 – Invalidated California law requiring pregnancy counseling clinics (including religious-based clinics) to provide information about free or low-cost clinics and abortion and family planning services; also required unlicensed clinics to inform patients of that status. Court ruled that the law was a violation of the First Amendment in that it constituted compelled speech.

Near v. Minnesota, 1931 – Near was publisher of Saturday Press in Minneapolis. He attacked corruption in government, claiming Jewish gangsters were in control of gambling and bootlegging and accused local officials of failing to act. The Minnesota Gag Law allowed courts to declare any obscene, lewd, lascivious, malicious or defamatory publication a public nuisance and stop publication. It was enforced against Near. USSC declared the law unconstitutional. Said prior restraint unacceptable except in unusual circumstances (war, national security, obscenity, etc.) PRESS SHOULD BE

PUNISHED AFTER THE FACT WITH LIBEL
LAWS.

Packingham v. North Carolina, 2017 – ruled that a
North Carolina law prohibiting convicted sex
offenders from accessing social media websites was an
unconstitutional infringement on the First Amendment
right of free expression.

Pentagon Papers, *NY Times v. U.S., 1971* – famous
though not significant in terms of precedent
importance. A test of prior restraint regarding national
security. Involved NY Times & Washington Post
publication of stolen papers relating to the
government's decision-making process in Vietnam.
Gov. stopped publication and case went to SC. Using
the preferred position doctrine, which presumes the
expression/speech to be constitutional (presumption of
constitutionality) unless proven otherwise, the Court
ruled for the newspaper. The government was unable
to justify censoring publication.

People v. Kobe Bryant, 2004 – Colorado Supreme
Court upheld prior restraint on the publication of
information related to previous sexual activities of
Bryant's accuser. Several newspapers had received
the information through mistaken e-mails from a court
reporter. Said prior restraint is constitutional when it:
1. serves a government interest of the highest order 2.
is the narrowest possible order available to protect that
interest, and 3. is necessary to protect against an evil
that is great and certain

*Planned Parenthood v. American Coalition of Life,
2002* – while abstract advocacy of violence is

protected, threatening a person with violence is not. Speech may not be punished just because it makes it more likely that someone will be harmed at some unknown time in the future by an unrelated third party. First Amendment protects speech that encourages others to commit violence, unless the speech is capable of "producing imminent lawless action." In this case a groups of anti-abortion activists posted a website called Nuremberg Files in which it listed the names and addresses of abortion doctors and when one was killed or injured, marked through their names on the site. In deciding this case, the Court said the applicable test was this: Would a reasonable person foresee that the statement would be interpreted by those to whom it was communicated as a serious expression of intent to harm or assault? If so, it was a true threat.

Progressive Case, U.S. v. Progressive, 1979 – Progressive magazine scheduled for publication a freelance article "The H-Bomb . . . and How to Make It." Submitted to gov. for accuracy check. Went to court to stop publication. Progressive argued that all information was from public sources. Gov. argued composite classification. Potentially harmful material can be classified upon creation. Case became moot when a small newspaper in Wisconsin published a similar article.

R.A.V. v. St. Paul, 1992 – Robert Victora and other youth burned a cross on the lawn of a black family in St. Paul, Minnesota. In addition to the usual trespass, damage to property laws, the teenagers were charged under a St. Paul ordinance which forbid the display of a burning cross or Nazi swastika or any writing or picture that arouses the anger, alarm or resentment in others on the basis of race, color, creed, religion or gender –fighting words. The U.S. Supreme Court struck down the St. Paul ordinance because it was content based -- specifying particular words that relate to race, creed, gender or sexual preference, while allowing other words. Justice Scalia wrote that while it is permissible to attempt to stop fighting words, the law cannot be used to prohibit speakers from expressing views on "disfavored subjects." He called it unconstitutional viewpoint discrimination.

Reed v. Town of Gilbert, Arizona, 2015 – ruled that a town ordinance restricting the size, location, number and duration of directional signs (in this instance directions to church services) was a violation of the First Amendment. The Court noted that the restrictions were content based and required strict scrutiny.

Simon & Schuster v. Crime Victims Board, 1991 – Court ruled unconstitutional state laws designed to prevent persons who have committed crimes from unjustly profiting from their stories. Court said the NY law in question was content based in that it singled out income from works recounting crimes.

Schenck v. U. S., 1919 – Socialist Charles Schenck published pamphlets urging draft resistance. He was convicted (under sedition laws) and his conviction was upheld. In the ruling, Justice Oliver Wendell Holmes wrote that Schenck's publication would have been ok in normal times, but in a time of war constituted a "clear and present danger of substantive evil" to national security . . . thus, the clear & present danger doctrine.

Schwarzenegger/Brown vs. Entertainment Merchants Association, 2011 –invalidated a California state law, which restricted the sale of violent video games to minors. The Entertainment Merchants Association and the Entertainment Software Association filed suit in federal court, alleging that the law was an impermissible restriction of speech in violation of the First Amendment. The district court and the Ninth Circuit ruled in favor of Entertainment Merchants. California appealed, asserting that the First Amendment does not protect the sale of violent video games to minors and that California need not show a direct causal link between violent video games and physical or psychological harm in minors before restricting such sales. The USSC ruled the California law to be a violation of the First Amendment. The Supreme Court's decision affects minors' constitutional rights, the power of states to control which materials children are exposed to, and the expression in media with violent content.

Snyder v. Phelps, 2011 – ruled that the First Amendment protects fundamentalist church members who stage anti-gay protests outside military funerals. Decision favors members of the Westboro Church headed by Fred Phelps who regularly show up at military (and celebrity) funerals waving signs with slogans such as "God Hates Fags," "God Hates Fag Enablers," "Thanks God for Dead Soldiers," etc. They content that the deaths are punishment for America's increasing support of gay rights. Roberts wrote,

"Speech is powerful. It can stir people to action, move them to tears of both joy and sorrow, and – as it did here – inflict great pain. On the facts before us, we cannot react to that pain by punishing the speaker. As a nation, we have chosen a different course – to protect even hurtful speech on public issues to ensure that we do not stifle public debate."

Street v. New York, 394 U.S. 576 (1969) – After publicly burning an American flag and making defiant comments regarding the flag, Street was convicted of violating a New York statute making it a misdemeanor to "publicly mutilate, deface, defile, defy, trample upon, or cast contempt upon an American flag either by words or act." The Supreme Court reversed Street's conviction because his comments, considered a possible factor in his conviction, were constitutionally protected by the First Amendment. Emphasizing that the mere offensiveness of words does not strip them of constitutional protection, the Court again noted that fighting words must present an actual threat of immediate violence, not merely offensive content.

Stromberg v. California, 1931– ruled that a 1919 California statute banning red flags was unconstitutional because it violated the 1st and 14th Amendments to the U.S. Constitution. Yetta Stromberg was a nineteen-year-old member of the Young Communist League. The flag was used as a form of dissent and was displayed by Stromberg at a summer camp for working class children. This was the first case in which the Supreme Court struck down a state law under the First Amendment as applied to the state infringement by way of interpreting the Fourteenth Amendment.

Terminiello v. Chicago, 1949 – speech cannot be banned because an audience may become offended, even violent . . . thus dismissing the heckler's veto . . . the speech can be banned if the speaker intends to provoke violence, but not simply because the audience is particularly sensitive. Justice William Douglas wrote, "Speech is often provocative and challenging. It may strike at prejudices and preconceptions and have profound unsettling effects as it presses for acceptance of an idea."

Texas v. Johnson, 1989 - flag burning case in which Johnson was convicted under Texas flag desecration law. Court determined that the law was aimed at the expressive nature of the act of burning a flag, rather than at the conduct itself, and thus had to meet a strict scrutiny test. They found no compelling justification for banning the burning of a flag. Ruled that Gregory Lee Johnson's flag burning demonstration outside Republican National Convention in Dallas was an acceptable form of communications. Justice Brennan wrote: "If there is a bedrock principle underlying the First Amendment, it is that government may not prohibit the expression of an idea simply because it finds it offensive or disagreeable."

Tinker v. Des Moines, 1969 – Symbolic speech. Students wore black arm bands to school protesting the Vietnam War. They were suspended from school. They argued that the arm bands were a form of expression protected by the First

Amendment. Supreme Court agreed. Said students do no lose their First Amendment rights just because they are in school. However, the court did say that any action, which disrupts (substantial disruption/ interference with school activities), could be restrained. Tinker used as precedent in 2003 ruling, Barber v. Dearborn Public Schools, the "Bush/International terrorist" case.

U.S. v. Eichman/U.S. v. Haggerty, 1990 – The two defendants burned flags to protest the passing of the Flag Protection Act. They were immediately arrested. Court, 5-4, struck down Flag Protection Act as unconstitutional, noting that flag burning was an act of free expression and thus protected by the First Amendment. Justice Brennan wrote, "Punishing desecration of the flag dilutes the very freedom that makes this emblem so revered, and worth revering."

U.S. v. O'Brien, 1968 – O'Brien burned draft card to protest Vietnam War in violation of federal statute making it a crime to knowingly destroy draft cards. Court determined that the federal restriction of expressive conduct could be upheld as long as the law:

> 1. was not intended to suppress expression
> 2. involved a substantial gov. interest (intermediate scrutiny)
> 3. was no greater than necessary to achieve that interest

In making the ruling, the Court reasoned that the law (draft card law) was not intended to suppress speech, but rather to properly maintain a Selective Service system.

U.S. v. Schwimmer, 1929 – Rosika Schwimmer was a pacifist who would not take the oath of allegiance to become a naturalized citizen. She was born in Hungary and while in the United States delivering a lecture she decided that she wanted to become a US citizen. When asked if she would be willing to "take up arms in defense of her country" she responded in the negative. She stated that she believed in the democratic ideal, but she asserted that she was an uncompromising pacifist. The Court held in a 6–3 decision that citizenship should be denied.

U.S. v. Stevens, 2010 – The Supreme Court invalidated a U.S. law that prohibited "knowingly selling depictions of animal cruelty with the intention of placing those depictions in interstate commerce for commercial gain." Stevens' conviction stemmed from an investigation into the selling of videos related to illegal dog fighting. With Chief Justice John G. Roberts writing for the majority, the Court reasoned that depictions of animal cruelty are not categorically unprotected by the First Amendment.

Virginia v. Black – 2003 - Asks if Virginia anti-cross burning law violates 1st Amendment. Under Virginia law, it is a felony "for any person or persons, with the intent of intimidating any person or group of persons, to burn or cause to be burned, a cross on the property of another, a highway or other public place . . . any such burning of a cross shall be prima facie (pry-muh fa-she) evidence of an intent to intimidate a person or group of persons." The SC ruled that a state has the right to ban cross burning done with the intent to intimidate (signals impending violence), but said the prima facie (pry-muh fa-she) evidence provision is unconstitutional . . . still may burn a cross for ceremonial purposes.

Defines True Threat as when:
1. It targets an individual or small group
2. It is intended to convey a real threat of impending physical harm
3. It is intended to arouse pervasive fear of violence in targeted individuals

Walker v. Texas Division, Sons of Confederate Veteran, 2015- ruled that the state of Texas did not violate the First Amendment by refusing to allow a specialty license plate with an illustration of a confederate battle flag. Justice Breyer, for the 5-4 majority, wrote that the plates constituted government speech and thus were immune from First Amendment attacks

Watts v. U.S., 1969 – Petitioner's remark during political debate at small public gathering that if inducted into Army (which he vowed would never occur) and made to carry a rifle "the first man I want to get in my sights is L. B. J.," held to be crude political hyperbole, which in light of its context and conditional nature did not constitute a knowing and willful threat against the President.

West Virginia State Board of Education v. Barnette, 1943 – the U.S. Supreme Court ruled that a West

Virginia requirement to salute the flag violates the free-speech clause of the First Amendment.

Whitney v. California, 1927 – Upheld the conviction under the California Criminal Syndicalism Act of Charlotte Whitney for her membership in the pro-violence Communist Labor Party, which advocated the overthrow of the U.S. government. In citing the clear & present danger test, the court went even farther by stating that the government could punish "utterances inimical to the public welfare, tending to incite crime, disturb the public peace, or endanger the foundations of organized government and threaten its overthrow."

Wynar v. Douglas County School District, 2013 – The 9th Circuit Court of Appeals upheld the school district's suspension of student Landon Wynar for violence-based posts on MySpace in which he had talked about how much ammunition would be needed to kill more people that the 32 victims at Virginia Tech in 2007, identifying specific people he planned to shoot and even setting a target date.

Yates v. U. S., 1957 – reversed the convictions of 14 members of the California Communist Party under the Smith Act (1939 act outlawing speech that advocated either forceful overthrow of the government or disloyalty among members of the military). In the decision, the Court ruled that the prosecution has failed to distinguish between the advocacy of abstract ideas (protected) and the advocacy of specific illegal action (not protected)

Libel

Bryson v. News America Publications, Inc.,
1991– short story published in Seventeen magazine
referred to a teenage character named "Bryson" as a
"slut." A former high school classmate of the author
with the last name of Bryson sued the magazine for
defamation. "The fact that the author used the
plaintiff's actual name makes it reasonable that third
persons would interpret the story as referring to the
plaintiff despite the fictional label," the Supreme Court
of Illinois wrote.

Carter-Clark v. Random House, Inc., 2005 – a New
York trial court rejected a libel plaintiff's defamation
claim against the publisher saying that "For a fictional
character to constitute actionable defamation, the
description of the fictional character must be so closely
akin to the real person claiming to be defamed that a
reader of the book, knowing the real person, would
have no difficulty linking the two. Superficial
similarities are insufficient."

Cubby v. CompuServ Inc., 1991 – early cyber-libel
case in which it was ruled that the ISP (CompuServ)
was not responsible for allegedly libelous statements
made by a third party and posted on its online
forum. CompuServ argued and the court agreed that it
was an electronic distributor, not a publisher and
therefore not liable.

Curtis v. Butts/AP v. Walker, 1967 – applies the actual
malice rule to public figures; and established the test

for reckless disregard for the truth – urgency, source reliability, and probability.

Doe v. Cahill, 2005 – ruled that an anonymous blogger need not be revealed unless the plaintiff can establish likelihood of prevailing in a defamation suit.

Edwards v. National Audubon Society, Inc., 1977 – established the neutral reporting privilege. Ruling stated that when a responsible, prominent organization makes a charge against a public figure, the media are protected in reporting the accusations regardless of the reporter's private views about the accuracy of the accusations. The fact that such allegations are being made is newsworthy and protected. Concept has not been widely accepted by the courts.

Fair Housing Council v. Roommates, 2008 – helps to clarify the distinction between user generated content v. internet service provider produced content. Good Samaritan provision applies only to sites hosting user generated content. In the Fair Housing case, the site matched renters with those looking to rent and required answers to specific questions in order to create user profiles. Because the site's questions shaped the content, the court ruled it more than a passive distributor and thus not protected by 230 immunity.

Gertz v. Welch, 1974 – Elmer Gertz was retained by a Chicago family to bring civil action against a policeman who had shot and killed their son. Policeman had already been convicted of second degree murder. American Opinion magazine (Welch was publisher) ran an article saying Gertz was responsible for a frame-up of the policeman, that he was part of a Communist conspiracy to discredit local police, that he was a Leninist and a Communist. A jury found American Opinion guilty of libel per se & awarded Gertz $50,000. Court of Appeals ruled that because the American Opinion article concerned a matter of public concern (Rosenbloom), Gertz would have to show actual malice. Supreme Court reversed Rosenbloom saying private persons should not have to show actual malice as they do not have the same opportunity for rebuttal as public officials and public figures do. S.C. added that while private persons should not have to show actual malice to win, some form of fault should be required (to be set by states). Suggested a minimum of simple negligence or acting without reasonable care. S.C. then said that while private persons would not need to show actual malice to win a suit, such proof would be required in order to win punitive damages. S.C. decision also established two public figure categories:

> 1. All purpose or total public figure – someone with pervasive fame.
> 2. Limited public figure – someone who has voluntarily thrust self into a public controversy with the intent to influence the outcome of that controversy.

GW Equity v. Xcentric Ventures, 2009 – involved a website where the public could post negative impressions of various businesses. Monitors did review posts and removed comments deemed offensive. Plaintiff argued that since the website was actively engaged in shaping content and therefore should not be protected by 230 (Good Samaritan provision), that the act was not intended to provide absolute immunity. Court ruled that Xcentric did not provide substantial editorial control and thus was protected under 230.

Harte-Hanks Communications, Inc. v. Connaughton, 1989 – ruled that a newspaper's "deliberate" failure to verify damaging information constituted reckless disregard for the truth. The court said that while failure to investigate alone would not support a finding of actual malice, "the purposeful avoidance of the truth is in a different category."

Hepps v. Philadelphia Inquirer, 1986 – ruling that changed the burden of proof requirement in libel law. Ruled that an individual suing the media for a damaging statement involving a matter of public concern is responsible for proving the statement false. Prior to this ruling, defendants in libel cases had to prove the truth of their statement(s).

Herbert v. Lando, 1979 – ruled that in order for plaintiffs to prove actual malice they may inspect a writer's notes and require answers to detailed questions to determine defendant's actual state of mind during the editorial process.

John Peter Zenger Trial – Zenger printed the New York Weekly Journal that attacked the royal governor of NY, William Cosby. Cosby had Zenger prosecuted for seditious libel. In the famous trial in 1735, Zenger's attorney Andrew Hamilton argued that the criticisms of Cosby were accurate (truth as a defense). While the judge ruled such an argument irrelevant (truth was not a defense under the law at that time), Hamilton appealed to the jurors to make up their own minds and to free Zenger if they believed his statements about Cosby to be accurate. The jury reacted by siding with Zenger, finding him not guilty. While it did not officially change the law, it had the effect of discouraging similar suits.

Masson v. The New Yorker, 1991 – SC court ruled that altering the words in a quotation does not equate with knowledge of falsity, unless the alteration results in a material change in the meaning conveyed by the statement.

Milkovich v. Lorain Journal – 1991 – ruled that a statement, which has a factual connotation or which implies an assertion of object fact is not an opinion. In Milkovich, the assertion that someone had lied was ruled a statement of fact and not opinion. Writing for the Court, Chief Justice William Rehnquist said that "an expression of opinion may often imply an assertion of objective fact." He added that couching the accusation in such terms as "In my opinion, Jones is a liar," can cause as much damage to one's reputation as simply saying "Jones is a liar."

New York Times v. Sullivan, 1964 – public officials must show actual malice, actual malice defined as knowledge of falsity or reckless disregard for the truth. Justice Brennan: Free expression needs breathing space to survive. Ruling was the first step in doing away with strict liability – previous concept, which meant the defendant was responsible for the harm regardless of the cause. Brennan wrote, "Thus we consider this case against the background of a profound national commitment to the principle that debate on public issues should be uninhibited, robust and wide-open, and that it may well include vehement, caustic, and sometimes unpleasantly sharp attacks on government and public officials."

Ollman v. Evans – 1984 – ruled that it was an expression of opinion for columnists to have termed a college professor a Marxist and also to have said that a colleague rated him as having low status in his field. In determining that the statements in question were opinion, the court said that to be factually based the statements would have to be characterizable as either true or false.

Rosenbloom v. Metromedia, 1967 – A Metromedia radio station broadcast news stories about Rosenbloom's arrest for possession of obscene literature and the police seizure of "obscene books," using terms such as "smut literature racket" and "girlie-book peddlers." When he was acquitted Rosenbloom filed a libel suit against Metromedia. The jury found for petitioner and awarded damages. The Court of Appeals reversed, holding that the New York Times Co. v. Sullivan standard applying proof of actual malice applied. They said that although he was not a public figure, his involvement in an activity of public or general interest required proof of actual malice.

Stratton Oakmont, Inc. v. Prodigy Services Co., 1995 – cyber-libel ruling in which the ISP (Prodigy) was determined to be liable for defamatory statements published on its site because it had advertised to the public that it controlled the content of its bulletin boards and, in fact, screened out some content, therefore assuming the role of publisher rather than simply distributor. The obvious implication of the two cases involving CompuServ and Prodigy was that ISPs should keep their hands-off content in order to avoid trouble. Concerned that these rulings would lead to more offensive content, Congress included the Good Samaritan provision in the 1996 Telecommunications Act. The provision stipulated that providers of interactive computer services would be treated as distributors rather than publishers even when providing monitoring/editing of content.

Time v. Firestone, 1976 – Time magazine published a notice of the divorce of Russell Firestone from his wife on grounds of extreme cruelty and adultery. (Divorce was actually granted on the grounds that neither party was domesticated. Mrs. Firestone sued for libel. Time argued that she was a public figure because of all the publicity surrounding the divorce and that she should have to show actual malice. Court ruled that public controversy does not equate to public interest, that she did not voluntarily thrust herself into a public controversy, and that she would not have to show actual malice.

Zeran v. America Online, 1998 – Court interpreted the Good Samaritan provision as providing total distributor/publisher immunity for ISPs: The provision "precludes courts from entertaining claims that would place a computer service provider in a publisher's role." While the total immunity stance has largely prevailed, some courts have returned to a traditional approach of requiring publisher responsibility.

Privacy

Bollea v. Gawker, 2016 – Florida trial case involving an online website's (Gawker) First Amendment rights vs. Hulk Hogan's (Terry Gene Bollea) claim of 4th Amendment right of privacy. The case resulted from Gawker's posting portions of a secretly recorded sex tape of Bollea having sex with the wife of one of his friends. After months of back and forth motions, a trial verdict awarding Bollea $140 million in damages, and promises of appeal, the case ended in a $31 million settlement. While the publicity-heavy case created minimum if any legal precedent, it did result in the shutting down of the Gawker.com website.

Booth v. Curtis Publishing Company, 1962 – a photograph of actress Shirley Booth that had been used in Holiday Magazine as part of a feature (news) display was subsequently published in advertisements as illustration of typical magazine content for the purpose of attracting advertisers and subscribers. Booth sued claiming appropriation for advertising purposes. The USSC ruled that publications could use photographs previously used in an editorial context to advertise their publication.

Byrd v. United States, 2018 – Court held that the driver of a rental car whose name does not appear on the rental agreement, but who has the renter's permission, has a reasonable expectation of privacy;

and that a police officer may not search the vehicle without a search warrant. To do so would be a violation of the Fourth Amendment.

Cantrell v. Forest City Publishing Company, 1974 – ruling involving actual malice in false light privacy case. Several months after the collapse of a bridge in which 44 people were killed, a reporter for the Cleveland Plain Dealer wrote a follow up on the impact of the disaster on the family of one of the deceased. The story stressed the poverty of the Cantrell family and the deteriorating condition of their home. Turns out much of the story was embellished. The Cantrells were awarded false light privacy damages.

Carpenter v. U.S., 2018 – ruled that the warrantless search of cell phone and cell tower information constitutes an invasion of the 4th Amendment. Charged with armed robbery based on information obtained from the search, Carpenter had moved to suppress the records arguing that a probable cause search warrant was required.

Collins v. Virginia, 2018 – A police officer must have a warrant to enter private property to search a vehicle parked a few feet from the house. Officer had lifted a tarp covering a motorcycle to identify it as having been involved in traffic law violations and as having been stolen. Ruled that the "automobile exception," which may apply in limited Fourth Amendment situations did not apply in this case.

Cox v. Cohn, 1971 – Court ruled that it is not an invasion of privacy to publish the name of a rape victim when that name is a part of public record during a trial; Florida Star v. B.J.F., 1989, extended to legally obtained information gotten from outside of court.

Dieteman v. Time Inc., 1971 – ruled that photos taken inside a private home w/o knowledge were an invasion of privacy. Cameras and voice recording devices are inconsistent with a person's expectation of privacy inside his/her home. Later rulings have differed when the facts involved secret recordings inside a place of business.

Florida v. Harris, 2013 – ruled 9-0 that police may search a motor vehicle on a public road for drugs once a properly trained police dog has alerted to a smell of drugs on a vehicle.

Florida v. Jardines, 2013 – ruled 5-4 that a dog sniff at the front door of a house where the police suspected drugs were being grown constitutes a search for purposes of the Fourth Amendment and is a violation without a search warrant.

Griswold v. Connecticut, 1965 – landmark privacy case favoring Planned Parenthood in which the USSC voided a Connecticut law that criminalized counseling or medical procedures directed at married couples for the purpose of preventing conception. The Court ruled that while there is no specific constitutional protection of privacy, guarantees in the Bill of Rights (1st, 3rd, 4th, and 9th) establish a right of privacy, including in marital relations.

Hustler v. Falwell, 1988 – re a fictitious interview with Rev. Jerry Falwell in which it was said that "his first time" was with his mother in an outhouse. Included a small disclaimer. Falwell sued for libel, invasion of privacy, and infliction of emotional distress. Judge dismissed the privacy claim but sent the libel and emotional distress cases to court. Jury dismissed the libel claim noting that it was so farfetched, no one would believe it was intended as the truth; but awarded $200,000 in emotional stress damages; U.S. Appeals Court upheld; U.S Supreme Court reversed. Rehnquist said that although most would consider it repugnant, it was satire and satirists must be protected. Said that in order to win an emotional distress claim, it would have to be shown:

> 1. That the parody or satire amounted to a statement of fact, not opinion.
> 2. That it was a false statement of fact.
> 3. That actual malice was involved.

Katz v. U.S., 1967 – ruled that the warrantless wiretapping of a phone booth allegedly used by Charles Katz to illegally transmit gambling information was an unreasonable violation of his 4th Amendment rights.

Lawrence v. Texas, 2003 – ruled that a Texas sodomy law, which criminalized sexual acts between same-sex couples, was an unconstitutional intrusion of individual privacy based on the due process clause of the 14th Amendment.

Leverton v. Curtis Pub. Co, 1951 – The *Saturday Evening Post* ran a photo of a child at an accident scene with a story of pedestrian carelessness. Accident had been fault of driver . . . therefore false light.

Maryland v. King, 2013 – ruled 5-4 that when officers make an arrest supported by probable cause to hold a suspect for a serious offense and bring him to the station to be detained in custody, taking and analyzing a cheek swab of the arrestee's DNA is, like fingerprinting and photographing, a legitimate police booking procedure that is reasonable under the Fourth Amendment.

Midler v. Ford, 1988 - Bette Midler won a suit against Ford Motor under the appropriation of name or likeness for commercial purpose category when Ford used a voice impersonator to make it sound as if she were singing an commercial to the tune of her "Do You Want to Dance." Court ruled that a popular singer's voice is part of her identity and may not be imitated without her consent.

Pavesich v. New England Mutual Life Insurance Co., 1905 - Atlanta artist Paolo Pavesich sued when his photo was used in a newspaper ad representing a happy, contented person with insurance. Georgia became the first state to recognize the right of privacy in common law when they awarded Pavesich $25,000 in personal damages due to the invasion.

Riley v. California, 2014 – ruled 9-0 that police must have a search warrant before searching the contents of a cell phone belonging to an individual who has been arrested, saying the Fourth Amendment protects individuals from unwarranted and unreasonable government intrusion.

Roberson v. Rochester Folding Box Company, 1902 –
Abigail Roberson's picture was reproduced on 25.000
copies of a poster advertising. She sued, but lost her
case when the New York court ruled that there was no
law of privacy. But the case generated such public
outrage that the NY legislature passed the first
statutory law of privacy making it illegal to use one's
name or likeness for advertising or trade purposes
without consent.

Time v. Hill, 1967 – requires proof of actual malice
(knowledge of falsity or reckless disregard for the
truth) in a false light privacy case. Hills held hostage;
book Desperate Hours written, stretching the facts;
play based on book; magazine coverage of play related
to Hill family, took photo in front of their house. etc.
etc.

U.S. v. Jones, 2012 – ruled that the placing of a gps
device on a privately-owned vehicle constituted a
search and thus was an invasion of the owner's
privacy. Although police had obtained a 30-day
warrant for a specific geographical area, the device
was placed on the vehicle after the warrant had expired
and was used to follow the car beyond the specified
area.

Zacchini v. Scripps-Howard Broadcasting, 1977 –
ruled that appropriation law can apply to news content
in rare cases. In this instance, a local television station
taped Zacchini's human cannonball act an Ohio county
fair and aired the 15 second act. Zacchini sued
claiming the station had appropriated his professional
property and threatened the future economic value of

his act. Court held for Zacchini stating that First Amendment privilege did not apply as entire act was broadcast without consent. Considered a narrow ruling. General rule remains that appropriation involves taking for commercial purpose and that use in a news context is exempt.

Access to Places & Information

Food Lion v. Capital Cities/ABC, 1999 – reporters in NC went undercover at a Food Lion to follow up on claims the store was selling old/spoiled meat. Original award of $5 million eventually became $2 - $1 for trespass, and $1 for not being a loyal employee.

Hanlon v. Berger, 1999, Wilson v. Layne, 1999 - both involved cases in which law enforcement officers invited reporters/photographers to accompany them on arrests (Layne) or gathering evidence (Hanlon) on private property. Does not apply to ride-alongs etc. in public places.

Houchins v. KQED, 1975 – similar to Pell and Saxbe, an inmate in a California jail committed suicide, and a psychiatrist's report said the jail conditions may have contributed to the suicide. KQED TV requested permission to film in the part of the jail where the inmate resided, but the sheriff refused. They were offered a regular jail tour, the same tour offered the general public. However, it did not include the portion of the jail where the suicide had taken place. KQED argued that it had a constitutional right to gather information and challenged the restriction. SC Decision: Neither the First nor Fourteenth

Amendments mandate a right of access to governmental information or sources of information within governmental control. NOTE: the decision does not preclude access, just leaves it up to the prison superintendent.

Miller v. National Broadcasting Co., 1986 – California Court of Appeals ruling asserting that a reporter who had accompanied paramedics into a private home, filming resuscitation attempts on a heart attack victim, had failed to obtain permission from the homeowner (wife of victim). Court ruled that the wife could sue for trespass as well as invasion of privacy.

Oak Tree v. Ah King, 1989 – in a similar decision, court ruled that police may ban a reporter from the scene of an airplane crash in a non-public area of a county airport. "Journalists have a right to gather news by any means within the law, but do not have a First Amendment right of access, solely because he/she is a newsgatherer, to the scene or an airplane crash where the general public has been excluded."

Pell v. Procunier, 1974, and *Saxbe v. Washington Post, 1974* – in separate cases reporters requested but were refused the right to interview specific prisoners ..... both were told they could tour prison facilities and even talk with prisoners at random, but could not interview specific prisoners. Media argues the denial was a violation of First Amendment rights. SC Decision: Reporters have no constitutional right of access to prisons or their inmates beyond that afforded the general public. Press have the right to print whatever they can get, but government has no obligation to provide legal access beyond that given the general public.

Youngstown Pub. Co. v. McKelvey, 2005, and *Baltimore Sun v. Ehrlich, 2004* – there is no special right of 1st Am. access to interview or speak with politicians in one-on-on situations. Gov. employees may pick/discriminate re which reporters they want to talk to.

Wilson v. Layne, 1999, and *Hanlon v. Berger, 1999* - both involved cases in which law enforcement officers invited reporters/photographers to accompany them on arrests (Layne) or gathering evidence (Hanlon) on private property. Does not apply to ride-alongs etc. in public places.

Zemel v. Rusk, 1964 – one of the earlier cases addressing the issue of information gathering, a U.S. citizen is denied a passport to go to Cuba to gather information. Chief Justice Earl Warren wrote: the right to speak and publish does not include the right to gather information.

Media & the Justice System

Bruno Hauptman criminal trial, 1935 – Bruno Richard Hauptman was on trial for murdering the 20-month old son of Charles Lindberg, who had become an American hero in May 1927, by making the first solo trans-Atlantic flight, from New York to Paris. Because of the wide-spread media attention to the trial and the circus-like atmosphere that prevailed, the American

Bar Association responded by implementing Canon
35, a ban on cameras in the courtroom.

Chandler v. Florida, 1981 – ruled that cameras do not
prevent a fair trial and that states may allow their
presence in the courtroom. If a state allows cameras,
their presence does not violate the constitutional
guarantee of a fair trial. If a state denies cameras, it is
not a violation of the First Amendment.

Estes v. Texas, 1965 – SC ruled that the First
Amendment did not give the press the right to take
photographs during a trial, but did say that at some
point in the future when technology was not so
obtrusive it might be allowed. Decision said:

   1. Cameras interfere with jury - pressure due to
   exposure.
   2. Interfere with witnesses - intimidating.
   3. Impact on judge - burden of control.
   4. Impact on defendant - harassment.

Gannett v. Des Pasquale, 1979 – Supreme Court
upheld an order banning a reporter from a pre-trial
hearing . . . resulting in an avalanche of closings, and
disagreements on the part of the justices re the
interpretation.

Globe Newspapers v. Superior Court, 1982 – Struck
down a Massachusetts state law that required closure
of trials during testimony of juvenile victims of sexual
offenses. Said trial closure would need to meet strict
scrutiny standards: compelling government interest,
narrowly tailored for a specific situation. Note that
this decision does not require open testimony in these

cases, simply says a state law cannot mandate closure under any and all situations.

Irvin v. Dowd, 1961 – murder conviction and death sentence of Irvin was reversed due to what the court described as a "pattern of prejudice" created by extensive newspaper and broadcast coverage. Although 268 potential jurors were released for having fixed opinions about his guilt, the 12 selected had all indicated that they assumed Irvin was guilty. Following the reversal, he was retried, found guilty and sentenced to life imprisonment.

KQED v. Vasquez, 1991 – federal court upheld the prohibition on television coverage of executions.

Nebraska Press Association v. Stuart, 1976 – trial of a man charged with six murders, restricted information during pre-trial, later only restricted confession. SC ruled that the restrictive (gag) orders were unconstitutional, saying . . . There must be a clear and present danger to defendant's rights in order for such an order to be allowed.

> There must be evidence to reasonably conclude that:
> 1. There will be intense and pervasive publicity about the case
> 2. No other measure (change of venue etc.) would work.
> 3. The order will in fact prevent prejudicial publicity.

Press Enterprise v. Riverside Superior Court, 1984 – ruled that the public and the press have the right to attend the voir dire process. Press Enterprise v. Riverside Superior Court, 1986 - opened pre-trial hearing except when . . .1. It is proven that there is substantial probability that the defendant's right to a fair trial will be prejudiced by publicity.2. A reasonable alternative to closure cannot protect defendant's rights.

Richmond Newspapers v. Virginia, 1980 – case the SC heard to clarify the ruling in Gannett. Overruled interpretation of Gannett as allowing closure of criminal trials. Said the public right to attend criminal trials is guaranteed by common law and the First Amendment. Requires extreme circumstances in order to close a criminal trial. Upholds interpretation of Gannett as allowing closure of pre-trial hearings.

Rideau v. State of Louisiana, 1963 – Rideau was accused of robbing a bank, kidnapping several bank employees, and killing one of them. During questioning by the local sheriff, he confessed while being filmed. A local TV station broadcast the confession repeatedly. During the pre-trial, Rideau's request for a change of venue was denied. He was convicted and sentenced to death. On appeal, the U.S. SC reversed the conviction claiming, "it was a denial of due process of law to refuse the request for a change of venue."

Sheppard v. Maxwell, 1966 - controversial trial in which conviction of Sheppard was overturned due to prejudicial publicity . . . in which decision criticized the judge for not controlling the courtroom. Sheppard was a wealthy doctor in the Cleveland suburb of Avon

Lake. His wife was killed while he was downstairs sleeping on the couch. He claimed he heard a noise, ran upstairs, fought with the assailant, was knocked unconscious by a figure huddled over his wife's bed. Press sensationalized Sheppard's affair with a nurse, quoted a judge as saying he was "guilty as hell," questioned why he had not been arrested and brought to trial, printed names of jurors and urged readers to call or write. Sheppard was convicted, overturned, re-tried, acquitted.

Confidential Sources

Branzburg v. Hayes, 1972 (also in re Pappas & U.S. v. Caldwell) – Branzburg was a reporter for the Louisville Courier-Journal. He did a story about making hashish from marijuana and about drug use in Frankfort County. He was called to testify before a grand jury, refused, and lost argument . . . appealed to USSC. RULING: Reporters do not have a right of confidentiality, no special privilege.

Cohen v. Cowles, 1982 - Dan Cohen offered information to reporters re a Democratic candidate for lieutenant governor. Reporter promised to not reveal Cohen's identity. The reporter's editor overruled her decision, citing a company policy, and printed the Cohen's name. Cohen sued for breach of contract . . . trial court awarded him $200,000 compensatory and $500,000 punitive under state laws re promissory estoppel. Minnesota Court of Appeals affirmed, but threw out punitive damages. Minnesota Supreme Court reversed the decision of the trial court. USSC reversed Minnesota Supreme Court ordering them to reconsider the promissory estoppel statute, noting that enforcement would not be a violation of the First Amendment. They then upheld the jury decision and the $200,000 award.

In a promissory estoppel case, the plaintiff must show:
1. defendant made a definite promise
2. defendant intended the promise and the plaintiff relied on the promise
3. upholding of the promise is required to prevent an injustice

Miller v. United States, 2005 – New York Times reporter Judith Miller jailed in 2005 on civil contempt charges for refusing to reveal confidential sources having to do with information never published (Valerie Plame case). She was released only after her source released her from the confidentiality agreement and the prosecutor agreed to limited testimony – D.C. district court and appeals court both upholding precedent, which says there is no First Amendment privilege protecting sources . . . USSC refused to hear. Prompted Congress to consider the Free Flow of Information Act . . . still not passed.

Risen v. U.S., 2013 – USSC refused to grant certiorari in an appeal from a 4th Circuit Court of Appeals in which the lower court had ordered Risen, a *New York Times* reporter, to comply with a subpoena requesting he identify a confidential source, the government believed was he source of a C.I.A. leak. The Justice Department eventually decided not to call Risen to testify.

U.S. v. Dickinson, 1972 – reporter ignored a judge's gag order and printed a story, reporter was cited for contempt, court of appeals struck down the judge's gag order but upheld the contempt citation. *(Dickinson Rule* - contempt citation may stand even though a court order which resulted in the citation is later ruled invalid. Not accepted in all jurisdictions.)

Zurcher v. Stanford Daily, 1978 – newsroom search case. Involved a confrontation between police and student demonstrators. Newspaper had photos of confrontation. Police searched the newsroom to get the negatives. Court ruled in a 5-3 decision that the search was OK . . . that it was not a First Amendment issue, but rather a 4th amendment (search) issue. Ruled that a search warrant can be issued to search any location where it is believed there can be found evidence of a crime. , , , even when it is a third party search involving a site where no one is suspected of criminal activity.

Copyright / Creative Property

A&M Records v. Napster, 2001 – Napster provided the framework for peer to peer file sharing through a central server. Court ruled it was a contributory infringer and shut it down.

Associated Press v. International News Service, 1919 – AP said INS was pirating its news. INS said the news dispatches were not copyrighted and thus were public domain. The Supreme Court ruled that while there were no property rights to the news, what INS was doing constituted unfair competition and was thus illegal.

Basic Books v. Kinko's, 1991 – ruled that Kinko's practice of copying articles and compiling them into custom textbooks to be sold to college students was an infringement.

Campbell v. Acuff-Rose Music, Inc., 1994 – parody case involving 2 Live Crew's parody of Roy Orbison's "Pretty Woman." SC supported the idea that the use was a parody protected by Fair Use even though a commercial.

Community for Creative Non-Violence v. Reid, 1989 – ruling involved copyright ownership of works for hire. Reid created a statue for CCNV, which after a scheduled display became the center of a disagreement involving creative ownership. Under a normal employee-employer arrangement (reporter writing stories at newspaper he/she works for), the employer owns the creative work. However, the question here is whether Reid was an employee of CCNV. Because Reid had used his own tools and had created the statue in his own studio, he was deemed an independent contractor rather than an employee.

Dr. Seuss Enterprises v. Penguin Books USA, 1996 – Penguin Books published a poetic account of the O.J. Simpson trial in a book titled, The Cat NOT in the Hat! A Parody by Dr. Juice. The 9th Circuit held that the book did not parody The Cat in the Hat, but simply retold the Simpson story. Therefore, there was no fair-use defense, and the book was deemed a copyright infringement.

Eldred v. Ashcroft – 2003 - U.S. Supreme Court upheld the Bono Copyright Term Extension Act which provided continued protection of copyrights held by companies such as Disney. Extended time limits by 20 years, life plus 50 years to life plus 70 years. Works for hire were extended to 95 years from publication or 120 years from creation.

Feist Publications v. Rural Telephone Service Co, Inc. (1991) – ruled that a list of names in a telephone directory is not copyrightable. Feist did not need permission to take names from Rural Telephone Service Company's directory and publish them in its own directory. Eliminated the "sweat of brow" argument. Labor invested to gather information does not give ownership when there is no original creation.

Greenburg v. National Geographic Society, 2001 – ruled that when the National Geographic published a CD-ROM of back issues of the magazine it violated the copyright ownership of a photograph originally licensed as a cover photo. The court ruled that use of the photo in a CD-ROM was not a mere revision of the original but rather a new collective work.

Harper & Row v. Nation, 1985 – ruled that Nation's publication of an excerpt from an unpublished book by Gerald Ford -- approx. 300 words about Ford's pardon of Nixon -- was not fair use. Based largely on right of first publication and the quality rather than quantity of the selection -- Ford's discussion of the controversial pardon was the heart of the book, the selling point.

Note: Many lower courts read the Harper & Row decision as precluding a fair use of unpublished materials, and in 1992 Congress amended the copyright law to read that the fact that a work is unpublished does not bar a finding of fair use.

Iancu v. Brunetti, 2019 – Ruled that language in the Lanham Act, which prevents the registration of a trademark that is considered "immoral" or "scandalous" is a violation of the Free Speech Clause of the First Amendment. Case resulted from Erik Brunetti's attempts to register his clothing brand "fuct."

Leibovitz v. Paramount Pictures Corporation, 1998 – Paramount did a teaser ad for the film, "Naked Gun: The Final Insult 33 1/3." The ad spoofed a 1991 cover of Vanity Fair, which featured a photo of a pregnant, nude Demi Moore. Paramount got another model, who was also pregnant, to pose nude. The head of Leslie Nielsen, the star of the film, was superimposed onto the body of the model. A federal district court and the 2nd U.S. Circuit Court of Appeals held that the parody ad was a fair use.

Matal v. Tam, 2017 – a trademark case involving the right of an Asian-American rock band to register its name, *The Slants*, under federal trademark law. When band leader Simon Tam attempted to register the band's name with the Federal Trademark office, he was refused based on a disparagement provision in the 1946 Lanham Act. Following a second denial by the office, he appealed to the U.S. Court of Appeals for the Federal Circuit, which found in favor of the band ruling that the disparagement clause was a violation of the First Amendment. The USSC accepted on appeal and upheld the ruling of the federal appeals court.

MGM Studios v. Grokster, 2005 – ruled that the act of distributing and promoting a product/software with the clear intent of fostering copyright infringement is liable for the resulting acts of infringement by others . . . inducement theory of contributory copyright infringement. This even though Grokster only provided software for users to share peer to peer.

Miller v. Universal Studios (1981) – ruled that facts/research/news are not copyrightable. Universal was not required to have Gene Miller's permission to use facts from his book in a docudrama. Copyright only protects the way a story is told, not the story itself -- the expression of the facts, not the facts.

Playboy Enterprises v. Frena, 1993 – Internet copyright case in which Frena operated a bulletin board service offering subscribers downloadable copies of photographs. When 170 copyrighted photos from Playboy magazine appeared on his site, Playboy sued for copyright infringement. The court ruled for Playboy, holding that Frena has usurped Playboy's right of distribution as well as its right of public display.

Rogers v. Koons, 1990 – upheld copyright holder's exclusive right to make derivative works from one's own creations, even in a different medium. Involved a sculpture created from a photograph that had been reprinted on notecards. The photographer sued the sculptor for copyright infringement and won.

Sony v. Universal Studios, 1984 – ruled that home videotaping for personal use only was not a violation of copyright and that Sony's sale of the Betamax for copying was not in violation of the copyright law . . . that time-shifting in the home is fair use.

Tasini v. New York Times, 2001 – ruled that when the Times and other newspapers provided articles originally published in the newspapers to the NEXUS data base, it was a use not covered under their copyright agreement with the freelance authors. The court agreed with the authors that the use constituted a separate publication for which they should be paid separately.

The Wind Done Gone – A 2001 copyright-infringement/parody case involved Alice Randall's novel, *The Wind Done Gone*, a parody of Margaret Mitchell's American classic, *Gone with the Wind*. Released in 2001, Randall's book used characters and scenes from Mitchell's original novel as a satirical critique of Mitchell's primitive depiction of African-Americans.

Mitchell's estate argued that Randall's novel borrowed too liberally from the original and was in essence a sequel, not a parody. A federal judge ordered an injunction against the publication of the book two months before it was to be released, but the injunction was lifted by the 11th Circuit on May 25 (SunTrust Bank v. Houghton Mifflin Co.).

Broadcast Licensing & Content

Adarand Constructors, Inc. v. Pena, 1997 – USSC ruled that race-based programs, state or federal, are constitutional only if they further a compelling governmental objective (strict scrutiny).

CBS v. FCC, 1981 – sustained candidate access rule re Carter-Mondale reelection campaign . . . "must give reasonable and good faith attention to access requests to any candidate for federal office . . . in order to refuse must cite realistic danger of substantial program disruption due to insufficient notice or excessive number of requests."

FCC v. Fox Television, 2009 – Court upheld the FCC's "fleeting expletives" policy of fining broadcasters for one-time spontaneous uses of curse words (the f-word and close cousins) . . . stems from incidents involving Bono, Cher, Nicole Ritchie etc. The decision did not address the First Amendment question relative to the policy, but simply says the FCC was not arbitrary or capricious under the Administrative Procedures Act in its enforcement of the policy. However, in 2010, the Second Circuit Court struck down the FCC regulations on First Amendment grounds for being "unconstitutionally vague, creating a chilling effect."

FCC v. Fox Television, 2012 – The Supreme Court held that the FCC's standards, as applied to the broadcasts were vague. The FCC did not give proper notice to broadcasters that they would be fined for fleeting expletives, so the practice violated due process. However, Justice Kennedy carefully noted that the Court did not decide whether the practice violated the First Amendment or that the indecency policy itself was unconstitutional. Only the way the policy was applied in this case was unconstitutionally vague.

FCC v. Pacifica (1978) – re George Carlin 's "7 Dirty Words" monologue . . . words you can't say on TV . . . FCC received one complaint from a listener and placed a warning/reprimand in Pacifica's file. Court and subsequent action by the FCC upheld censuring Pacifica and . . . distinguished indecency from obscenity, provided a definition for indecency as language which describes in terms patently offensive as measured by contemporary community standards for the broadcast medium, sexual or excretory activities and organs at times of the day when there is reasonable risk children may be in the audience. Established safe harbor for broadcasting indecency, now at 10 p.m. - 6 a.m.

Metro Broadcasting, Inc. v. FCC, 1990 – Court ruled that granting preference to license applicants who are racial minorities does not violate the Fifth Amendment guarantee of due process and equal treatment by government. In the narrow 5-4 ruling, Justice William Brennan wrote that "Safeguarding the public's right to receive a diversity of news and information over the airwaves is . . . an integral component of the FCC's mission."

Miami Herald v. Tornillo, 1974 – Miami Herald ran an editorial opposing Tornillo's political candidacy. He requested space for rebuttal and was refused. He sued under Florida's right of reply law . . . Supreme Court ruled the Florida right of reply law unconstitutional. No access to newspapers.

National Broadcasting Co. v. United States, 1943
– the U.S. Supreme Court states that no one has a First Amendment right to a radio license or to monopolize a radio frequency.

Prometheus v. FCC, 2004 – Appeals Court decision denied FCC regulation relaxing ownership rules, which had attempted to take national TV ownership limit to 45 percent. USSC denied cert, leaving the appeals court decision intact.

Red Lion v. FCC, 1969 – upheld the personal attack rule when Red Lion radio refused to give author Fred Cook reply time to answer a right-wing commentator who attacked Cook for criticizing Goldwater. Ruled that the station has to provide response time and that the person responding may not be required to pay for the time.

Syracuse Peace Council v. FCC, 1989 – U. S. Supreme Court decision upholding the right of the FCC to repeal the Fairness Doctrine, an FCC policy that had required broadcasters to provide balanced coverage of controversial issues in their communities.

Trinity Methodist Church v. Federal Radio Commission, 1932 – upheld FRD decision not to renew the radio license of the Rev. Bob Shuler. Aired two nights weekly in Los Angeles, Shuler regularly attacked government officials, making outlandish accusation of criminal activity etc. Also, made accusations about Jews and Catholics. Poses an interesting contrast with the 1931 decision in Near v. Minnesota in which the courts protected Nears right to make similar accusations in a print medium.

UCC v. FCC (United Church of Christ) 1966 – ruled that listening groups have "standing" to participate in a renewal hearing. . . . resulted from practices by station WLBT in Jackson, Mississippi, which supported segregation/refused to broadcast viewpoints supporting racial integration. . . many complaints made. UCC petitioned to challenge WLBT's license renewal and were told it did not have "standing," and the FCC issued a one-year renewal. Went to court and in the first UCC ruling, FCC was told to allow UCC standing and to reconsider. They then held a hearing in which UCC was allowed to participate, and issued a 3-year license . . . in a second case:

UCC v. FCC, 1969 – Court reversed FCC, vacated WLBT's license and ordered the FCC to invite applicants . . . went to Tugaloo College . . . became a leader in its market.

U.S. v. Southwestern, 1968 – FCC has authority to regulate cable (even though not specifically granted in its right to regulate television, the right to regulate television includes the right to regulate ancillary services.

Obscenity & Indecency

Ashcroft v. Free Speech Coalition, 2002 – ruled as invalid that part of the Child Pornography Prevention Act [CPPA] of 1996, which banned the sale and distribution [including internet] of materials, which appear to depict minors performing sexually explicit acts . . . including computer/electronic generated images. Child pornography must involve actual children / not virtual or computer generated children. [While the original was intended to prevent the exploitation of children, the rationale for including computer images was to protect children from pedophiles and child molesters who might be stimulated by such images. The act later was replaced by the PROTECT ACT [Prosecutorial Remedies and Other Tools to End the Exploitation of Children Today Act], which makes it illegal to send or receive an image that is indistinguishable from that of a minor in a sexual situation.

Ashcroft v. ACLU, 2002 /Gonzales v. ACLU, 2007 – ruled unconstitutional the Child Online Protection Act [COPA] (son of CDA), which had been passed by Congress in 1998, and intended to require identification for access to adult sites. It was enjoined and ruled unconstitutional by federal courts. Government appealed twice and was upheld by USSC both times.

Butler v. Michigan, 1957– limiting adults to that which was safe for children was unconstitutional, essentially doing away with the application of the Hicklin Rule.

Ginsberg v. New York, 1968 – established variable obscenity standards – says that states can distinguish between what is allowable for adults vs. what's ok for children, but must be careful in not limiting adults.

Hamling v. U.S., 1974 – jurors are to apply standards of the community and not base that standard on the most sensitive.

Jenkins v. Georgia, 1974 – affirms the application of the obscenity standard to materials determined to be hard-core.

Memoirs v. Massachusetts, 1966 – Fanny Hill case which, in conjunction with Roth, provided the Roth-Memoirs Test for obscenity:

>   1. The dominant theme of the material as a whole must appeal to the prurient interest in sex.
>   2. Court must find that the material is patently offensive because it affronts contemporary community standards relating to the description or representation of sexual matters.
>   3. Utterly without social value.

Miller v. California, 1973 – provides the current definition of obscenity:

>   1. An average person, applying contemporary local [not national] community standards, finds that the work, taken as a whole appeals to prurient interest.
>   2. The work depicts in a patently offensive way sexual conduct specifically defined by state law.
>   3. The work in question lacks serious literary, artistic, political, or scientific value.

New York v. Ferber, 1982 – relative to child pornography, provides that material which exploits children under 16 can be banned even if it does not meet the Miller test for obscenity. . . applies to live performances and depictions of live performances, not written or drawings.

Osborne v. Ohio, 1990 – allows prosecution of those who merely possess child pornography. Osborne distinguishes from the 1969 *Stanley v. Georgia* ruling that the Constitution protects private possession of otherwise unprotected speech [obscenity, not child pornography]. In the Stanley ruling, the court said that to tell someone what they could view or read in their own home was being paternalistic. Osborne targets child pornography as a means of protecting children from being exploited. If there's no market, children won't be used to create kid porn.

Paris Adult Theatre I v. Slaton, 1973 – upheld exclusion of obscenity from any First Amendment protection, refuting argument that material in question was being distributed only to willing adults.

Pinkus v. U.S., 1978 – children are not to be considered in determining community standards. Pope v. Illinois, 1987 – ruled that serious social value should be decided based on national rather than local standards and should be based on what a reasonable person would decide.

Pope v. Illinois, 1987 – Ruled that interpretation of the third part of the Miller definition of obscenity should be determined based on what a reasonable person would decide rather than on "contemporary community standards."

Reno v. ACLU, 1996 – ruled unconstitutional those portions of the Communication Decency Act [CDA], included in the 1996 Telecommunications Act, directed at indecent materials on the internet. Said only that which is obscene may be regulated. Distinguished from Pacifica, noting differences between broadcast and the Internet.

Roth v. U.S., 1957 – provided the first definitive ruling that obscenity is not protected by the First Amendment, and defined obscenity as that which to the average person applying contemporary community standards, the dominant theme of the material as a whole appeals to the prurient interest.

Sable Communications v. FCC, 1989 – ruled unconstitutional a revision of the Communications Act that banned erotic/sexual phone messages/services. Said could ban only obscene messages, that sexual expression that is indecent but not obscene is protected by the First Amendment. Said that a compelling interest would be required and that while there exists a compelling interest to protect children, a law must be narrowly constructed in order not to prevent legal expression from reaching consenting adults.

Stanley v. Georgia, 1969 – the U.S. Supreme Court ruled that the First and 14th Amendments protect a person's "private possession of obscene matter" from criminal prosecution. The Court noted that the state, although possessing broad authority to regulate obscene material, cannot punish private possession of such in an individual's own home.

U.S. v. Playboy Entertainment Group, Inc., 2002 – in distinguishing cable regulation from traditional broadcast regulation, Court ruled that provisions of the Telecom Act shielding basic cable subscribers from sexually oriented premium programming were unconstitutional. Opinion stated that such restrictions must be considered under strict scrutiny compelling interest standards.

U.S. v. American Library Association, 2003 – upheld the Children's Internet Protection Act [CIPA], which stipulates that public libraries cannot receive certain federal funds unless they install obscenity/child pornography blocking software on computers in public areas.

U.S. v. Williams, 2008 – upholds provisions of the PROTECT ACT, which makes it illegal to send or receive images online that are indistinguishable from that of a minor in a sexual situation, thus allowing the regulation of virtual or digitally created images to circumvent the holding of New York v. Ferber or the original intent of the Child Pornography Prevention Act.

Advertising/Commercial Speech

Bates v. Arizona, 1977 – ruled that state law prohibiting lawyers from advertising their services in any mass medium was a violation of the First Amendment.

Bigelow v. Virginia, 1975 – SC reversed the conviction of a newspaper editor for running an adv. offering abortion services, ruling that SPEECH DOES NOT LOSE ITS FIRST AMENDMENT PROTECTION JUST BECAUSE IT APPEARS IN THE FORM OF A COMMERCIAL ADVERTISEMENT.

Bolger v. Young's Drug Products Corp., 1983 – ruled that a company's mailings of unsolicited contraceptive pamphlets (in violation of federal law) promoting the use of condoms in general and its own product in particular constituted commercial rather than non-commercial speech. The court cited the following criteria in making a determination of commercial speech:

> 1.the company paid for the pamphlets
> 2.the pamphlets included references to a specific product
> 3.the company had an economic motive for mailing the pamphlets

Central Hudson Gas & Electric v. Public Service Commission of New York, 1980 – ruled unconstitutional a state ban on promotional advertising by electric utilities . . . opposed to policy of conserving energy. Concluded that commercial advertising is less protected than non-commercial speech. Provided the Central Hudson test:

Truthful advertising for legal goods and services may be regulated if:

> 1.the commercial message is misleading or related to unlawful activity
> 2.there is substantial state interest to justify
> 3.there is evidence that the regulation directly advances this interest.
> 4.there is a reasonable fit between the state interest and the governmental regulation. (must be narrow

enough to achieve desired result, but doesn't have to be the least restrictive means available).
5. In distinguishing between commercial speech and other forms of noncommercial speech, the court places restrictions on commercial speech at an intermediate scrutiny rather than strict scrutiny level, requiring only substantial state interest.

Greater New Orleans Broadcasting Association v. U.S., 1999 – ruled advertising legalized casino gambling within the state legal; said the ban violated the First Amendment because it "sacrifices an intolerable amount of free speech about lawful conduct.

Kasky v. Nike, Inc., 2002 – following news reports of Nike's exploitation of workers in overseas factories, Nike launched a public relations campaign refuting the allegations thru news releases and advertising. Under California statutes against misleading advertising a private citizen filed suit claiming the Nike ads contained false representations (in violation of the state law). The question was then whether or not Nike's "campaign" would be considered commercial speech (limited protection) or noncommercial speech (full protection under the First Amendment). The California court held that the Nike Communication was commercial speech, leaving it then up to a trial court to determine if the speech was misleading and therefore in violation of state law. Parties reached a settlement before a trial could be held.

44 Liquormart v. Rhode Island – 1996 - overruled a state law which forbid advertising the prices of liquor [law did not meet Central Hudson test]

Pittsburgh Press v. Pitts. Commission on Human Relations, 1973 – SC upheld the Commission's order that the Pitt. Press stop grouping "help wanted" classifieds as either "help wanted - Male" or "help wanted - Female," declaring the practice discriminatory based on sex. The newspaper used a First Amendment argument and the court did not reject such an argument as it had previously, but said simply that the decision was based on sexual discrimination . . . a small step toward recognizing advertising as a protected form of communications.

Reed v. Town of Gilbert, Arizona, 2015 – ruled 9-0 that an Arizona town had violated the First Amendment by placing size limits on signs announcing church services, while allowing different restrictions for political and directional signs; noted that such content based laws require strict scrutiny

Rubin v. Coors, 1995 – struck down a federal law, which forbid brewers from listing the alcohol content on labels [court said law did not meet the Central Hudson test]

Times v. Sullivan, 1964 – SC ruled that editorial/political advertising is within First Amendment protection. DID NOT INCLUDE COMMERCIAL ADVERTISING.

U.S. v. Edge Broadcasting Co., 1993 – ruled that a North Carolina station located on the Virginia border could be prevented from advertising the Virginia lottery under the "state interest" rationale.

Valentine v. Chrestensen, 1942 – SC upheld a local ordinance banning the distribution of advertising pamphlets (even with expression of opinion on backside), declaring that advertising was not protected by the First Amendment at that time.

Virginia State Board of Pharmacy v. Va. Citizens Consumer Council, 1976 – Ruled a violation of the First Amendment a Virginia law which prevented pharmacies from advertising the price of prescription drugs. The decision described advertising as a process of disseminating information and thus protected by the First Amendment. Clearly establishes that commercial speech has First Amendment protection. However, that right is limited and not equal to protection of political speech.

Freedom of Speech: Campaign Finance

Buckley v. Valeo, 1976 – "Reasonable restrictions" on individual, corporate, and group contributions to candidates were allowed; limits on campaign expenditures were unconstitutional since these placed "substantial and direct restrictions" on protected political expression.

Citizens United v. Federal Election Commission, 2010 – The Court struck down parts of the Bipartisan Campaign Reform Act, which put limits on corporate funding for campaigns from corporations and labor unions. The Court held that free speech was essential in a free society, and that speech was not less protected because the speaker was a corporation, labor union, or other organization. The Court upheld disclosure requirements for political advertising sponsors, and also kept in place a ban on direct contributions to candidates from corporations and unions.

Colorado Republican Federal Campaign Committee v. FEC, 1996 – The Court ruled that campaign spending by political parties on behalf of congressional candidates could not be limited as long as the parties work independently of the candidates.

McCutcheon v. Federal Election Commission, 2014 – invalidated under the First Amendment aggregate limits restricting how much money a donor may contribute to candidates for federal office, political parties, and political action committees saying such do not further the government's interest in preventing quid pro quo corruption or the appearance of such corruption, while at the same time seriously restricting participation in the democratic process.

McConnell v. Federal Election Commission, 2003 – Limitations on "soft-money" contributions and political advertisements were acceptable infringements of free speech because of the government's interest in preventing corruption or the appearance of corruption in elections.

Select Church-State Cases

Abington School District v. Schempp, 1963 – A Pennsylvania law requiring that each public school day open with Bible reading was struck down as violating the Establishment Clause.

Allegheny County v. Greater Pittsburgh ACLU, 1989 – A nativity scene with the words "Gloria in Excelsis Deo," meaning "Glory to God in the Highest," placed alone on the grand staircase of a courthouse endorsed religion and violated the Establishment Clause.

American Legion v. American Humanist Association, 1919 – Ruled that the display and maintenance of a large memorial cross by a local government does not violate the Establishment Clause of the First Amendment, also noting that the cross may have a historical significance beyond Christian symbolism.

Board of Education of Westside Community Schools v. Mergens, 1990 – The 1990 Equal Access Act, which required that public schools give religious groups the same access to facilities that other extracurricular groups have, was upheld. Allowing religious clubs to meet did not violate the Establishment Clause.

Braunfeld v. Brown, 1961 – The Court upheld a Pennsylvania law requiring stores to be closed on Sundays, even though Orthodox Jews claimed the law unduly burdened them since their religion required them to close their stores on Saturdays as well. The Court held that the law did not target Jews specifically as a group.

Burwell v. Hobby Lobby, 2014 – ruled 5-4 that corporations controlled by religious families cannot be compelled to pay for contraception coverage for female employees.

Cantwell v. Connecticut, 1940 – States could not require special permits for religious solicitation when permits were not required for non-religious solicitation. The Court began applying the Free Exercise Clause to the states and recognized an absolute freedom of belief.

Capitol Square Review and Advisory Board v. Pinette, 1995 – A cross placed by a private group in a traditional public forum adjoining the state house did not violate the Establishment Clause, as the space was open to all on equal terms.

Christian Legal Society v. Martinez, 2010 – The court ruled that a student organization at a public university was not free to limit their members to those who shared their belief system if that resulted in discrimination on the basis of sexual orientation.

Church of the Lukumi Babalu Aye v. City of Hialeah, 1993 – Laws passed by four Florida cities banning animal sacrifice were targeted as the Santeria religion, which employs animal sacrifice in prayer, and therefore the laws were unconstitutional.

Cutter v. Wilkinson, 2005 – A federal law prohibiting government from burdening prisoners' religious exercise did not violate the First Amendment's Establishment Clause.

Edwards v. Aguillard,.1987 – Louisiana could not require public schools that taught evolution to teach creationism as "Creation Science." The law had no secular purpose and endorsed religion, violating the Establishment Clause.

Elk Grove Unified School District v. Newdow, 2004 – A father challenged the constitutionality of requiring public school teachers to lead the Pledge of Allegiance, which has included the phrase "under God" since 1954. The Court determined that Mr. Newdow, as a non-custodial parent, did not have standing to bring the case to court and therefore did not answer the constitutional question.

Employment Division v. Smith, 1990 – Oregon could deny unemployment benefits to someone fired from a job for illegally smoking peyote during a religious ceremony. The Free Exercise Clause does not excuse people from obeying the law. Right of native Americans to use peyote was restored by Congress in the Religious Freedom Restoration Act in 1993.

Engel v. Vitale, 1962 – New York's requirement of a state-composed prayer to begin the school day was declared an unconstitutional violation of the Establishment Clause.

Epperson v. Arkansas, 1968 – An Arkansas law prohibiting the teaching of evolution was unconstitutional, because it was based on "fundamentalist sectarian conviction" and violated the Establishment Clause.

Everson v. Board of Education, 1947 – New Jersey's reimbursement to parents of parochial and private school students for the costs of busing their children to school was upheld because the assistance went to the child, not the church. This case also applied the Establishment Clause to the actions of state governments.

Goldman v. Weinberger, 1986 – Air Force penalties against a Jewish chaplain who wore a yarmulke (skull cap) on duty in defiance of regulations were upheld. The military's interest in uniformity outweighed the individual right to free exercise.

Gonzales v. O Centro Espirita Beneficiente Uniao do Vegetal, 2006 – The courts ruled unanimously in favor of a small religious group who had argued that the Religious Freedom Restoration Act of 1993 required that they be free to use hoasca—an illegal drug under the Controlled Substances Act—for religious purposes (RFRA had been passed to clarify the rights of Native Americans to use peyote in religious ceremonies). Chief Justice Roberts wrote that the Court had to review individual religious freedom claims and grant exceptions to generally-applicable laws.

Good News Club v. Milford Central School, 2001 – Religious clubs were allowed to meet in public schools after class hours as other clubs were permitted to do. Allowing religious clubs to meet did not violate the Establishment Clause.

Hein v. Freedom from Religion Foundation, 2007 – After the Bush Administration created the Office of Faith-Based and Community Initiatives for the purpose of allowing religious charity organizations to gain federal funding, the Court ruled that taxpayers cannot bring Establishment Clause challenges against programs funded by the executive office.

Holt v. Hobbs, 2015 – ruled that Arkansas corrections violated religious freedom rights of Muslim inmates by forbidding them to grow beards.

Kiryas Joel School District v. Grumet, 1994 – A New York law creating a special school district to benefit disabled Orthodox Jewish children was struck down because it benefited a single religious group and was not neutral to religion.

Lee v. Weisman, 1992 – Officially approved, clergy-led prayer at public school graduations led to subtle religious coercion, and violated the Establishment Clause.

Lemon v. Kurtzman, 1971 – The Court struck down a Pennsylvania law reimbursing religious schools for textbooks and teacher salaries. The decision held that a program does not violate the Constitution if:

1. it has a primarily secular purpose;
2. its principal effect neither aids nor inhibits religion; and
3. government and religion are not excessively entangled.

Locke v. Davey, 2004 – States could refuse to award scholarship funds to college students pursuing divinity degrees in preparation for the ministry. The denial of government funding for religious instruction was not a violation of free exercise.

Lynch v. Donnelly, 1984 – The Court upheld a nativity display among other symbols in a public park "to celebrate the Christmas holiday and to depict the origins of that holiday."

Marsh v. Chambers, 1983 – States had the right to hire a chaplain to open legislative sessions with a prayer or invocation. The traditional practice did not violate the Establishment Clause.

McCreary County v. ACLU, 2005 – Two large, framed copies of the Ten Commandments in Kentucky courthouses lacked a secular purpose and were not religiously neutral, and therefore violated the Establishment Clause.

McDaniel v. Paty, 1978 – A Tennessee law barring members of the clergy from public office was overturned because it directly targeted people because of their religious profession.

Minersville v. Gobitas, 1940 – The Court upheld a Pennsylvania flag-salute law, because "religious liberty must give way to political authority." This was reversed in West Virginia v. Barnette (1943).

Mitchell v. Helms, 2000 – The federal government could provide computer equipment to all schools—public, private, and parochial—under the Elementary and Secondary Education Act. The aid was religiously neutral and did not violate the Establishment Clause.

Mueller v. Allen, 1982 – The Court upheld Minnesota's extension of tax credits to parents for money spent on tuition, books, transportation, and other costs associated with private and religious schools. Because the tax credits did not have the effect of advancing religion, and government and religion were not excessively entangled, there was no Establishment Clause violation.

Murray v. Curlett, 1963 – A Maryland law requiring prayer at the beginning of each public school day was declared unconstitutional as a violation of the Establishment Clause.

Pleasant Grove v. Summum, 2009 – ruled that a city in Utah was not required to allow a monument depicting the Seven Aphorisms of Summum to be constructed in a city park even though the park was home to at least 11 other privately donated displays including a Ten Commandments monument. Majority decision noted that placement of displays in a public park is government speech and thus not subject to scrutiny . . . contrary to the traditional view that public parks are public forum.

Reynolds v. United States, 1879 – A federal law banning polygamy was upheld. The Free Exercise Clause forbids government from regulating belief, but does allow government to regulate actions such as marriage.

Santa Fe Independent School District v. Doe, 2000 – A public school district's policy of having students vote on a prayer to be read by a student at football games violated the Establishment Clause. The voting policy resulted in religious coercion of the minority by the majority.

Sherbert v. Verner, 1963 – The Court ruled that states could not deny unemployment benefits to a person for turning down a job because it required him/her to work on the Sabbath. Requiring a person to abandon their religious convictions in order to receive benefits was a violation of the Free Exercise Clause.

Stone v. Graham, 1980 – State laws mandating the display of the Ten Commandments in public school classrooms were declared unconstitutional as a violation of the Establishment Clause.

Thornton v. Caldor, 1985 – Private companies are free to fire people who refuse to work on any day they claim is their Sabbath, because the First Amendment applies only to government, not to private employers.

Torcaso v. Watkins, 1961 – A Maryland requirement that candidates for public office swear that they believe in God was a religious test and violated Article VI of the Constitution as well as the First and Fourteenth Amendments.

Town of Greece v. Galloway, 2014 – By a 5-4 majority the USSC held that the town of Greece did not violate the establishment clause in opening town board meetings with legislative prayer. The court noted that legislative prayer had been practiced by Congress since the framing of the Constitution and, thus, was not meant to be rejected by the establishment clause.

Trinity Lutheran Church v. Comer, of Columbia, Inc. v. Comer, 2017 –Ruled that the exclusion of a religion-based daycare and preschool from an otherwise neutral and secular aid program is a violation of the First Amendment's free exercise clause.

Van Orden v. Perry, 2005 – A 6-foot monument displaying the Ten Commandments donated by a private group and placed with other monuments next to the Texas State Capitol had a secular purpose and would not lead an observer to conclude that the state endorsed the religious message, and therefore did not violate the Establishment Clause.

Wallace v. Jaffree, 1985 – An Alabama law setting aside a moment for "voluntary prayer" and allowing teachers to lead "willing students" in a prayer to "Almighty God . . . the Creator and Supreme Judge of the world" in public schools was struck down. The law had no secular purpose and endorsed religion, violating the Establishment Clause.

Westside Community Board of Education v. Mergens, 1990 – high court determined that a school district violated the Equal Access Act by denying use of its facilities to a religious club, while allowing a chess club, a scuba diving club and other "noncurriculum related" groups to use school facilities.

Wisconsin v. Yoder, 1972 – The Court ruled that Amish adolescents could be exempt from a state law requiring school attendance for all 14- to 16-year-olds, since their religion required living apart from the world and worldly influence. The state's interest in students' attending two more years of school was not enough to outweigh the individual right to free exercise.

Zelman v. Simmons-Harris, 2002 – A government program providing tuition vouchers for Cleveland school children to attend a private school of their parents' choosing was upheld. The vouchers were neutral towards religion and did not violate the Establishment Clause.

Terms, Concepts & Theories

The following pages contain notes related to media law and ethics terms, phrases, concepts and theories. Its intent is to provide a guide to relevant content of a basic university-level media or communications law course.

As many such courses include both law and ethics, this document includes materials related to both. All terms are combined in a single listing, all of which appear in alphabetical order.

AAAAA

ABA – American Bar Association

Absolutist Theory – absolute or literal interpretation of the "no law" statement. Nothing should infringe on 1st Amendment rights. If other rights conflict, 1st takes priority.

ACLU – American Civil Liberties Union. In its own words: "For almost 100 years, the ACLU has worked to defend and preserve the individual rights and liberties guaranteed by the Constitution and laws of the United States." See https://www.aclu.org/ for additional information.

Actual Damages – in a libel award, damages for actual harm; harm (mental anguish and suffering, damage to reputation) must be demonstrated.

Actual malice – defined as knowledge of falsity or reckless disregard for the truth; level of fault required in libel suits by public officials and public figures; enunciated in New York Times v. Sullivan, 1964.

Ad hoc balancing Theory (Strategy) – (ad hoc = case at hand) balancing 1st Amendment freedoms against other rights on a case by case basis (i.e., free press v. fair trial etc.)

Administrative Rules (Quasi Law) – As the U.S. has grown and technology increased, Congress has created special agencies to deal with specific areas of expertise, i.e., SEC, FTC, FCC etc. They make "rules" under the power given them by Congress.

Admonition – a compensatory remedy intended to prevent jurors from being exposed to prejudicial publicity in which members of the jury are "admonished" or instructed not to ready about, discuss, or otherwise consume media related to the ongoing trial.

Advertising - any action, method, or device intended to draw the attention of the public to merchandise, to services, to persons, and to organizations. Includes trading stamps, contests, freebies, premiums and even product labels in addition to the more common forms. Also, includes internet advertising.

Agape - Judeo-Christian Concept of unselfish love, "love your neighbor as yourself" accepting a person's existence as it is; to love him or her as is . . .blind, non-discriminating love.

Alien & Sedition Acts of 1798 – Sedition law forbade false, scandalous and malicious publications against the U.S. government, Congress and the president. Was used to quiet Jeffersonian political newspapers that were attacking President Adams. Jefferson pardoned those who had been convicted under the law after he was elected in 1800. Expired in 1801.

Amendment to U.S. Constitution – see Constitutional Amendment.

Appellate Courts – law reviewing courts, consider whether or not the law has been properly applied in the trial court in light of the facts.

Appellate jurisdiction – cases appealed from other courts either by direct appeal or through a writ of certiorari. Most reach SC by way of a writ of cert, an order from the SC to a lower court that the records of the case be sent forward. Any party may request a writ as long as all possible legal remedies have been exhausted (i.e., a vagrant convicted by a municipal court with no direct appeal process may request a writ.) Four out of nine justices must vote to hear a case for a writ to be granted.

Areopagitica – speech written by 17the Century writer/poet John Milton protesting British licensing/censorship of the British press (printers); historically important defense of a free press. Forms basis of the marketplace of ideas theory.

Aristotle's Golden Mean – Theory that the moral virtue is a mean between two extremes. Journalistic independence, for example, might fall between the

extremes of "no involvement" to "anything goes."
Mean not necessarily the mathematical center, may
lean one way or another depending on the situation! In
hiring of minorities, for example, might lean to over
hiring in order to correct non-parity.

Ascertainment – to ascertain means to find out or
discover; in the context of broadcast regulation it
refers to a previous requirement that broadcast license
holders must ascertain the interests and needs of their
audiences and show that they are meeting those needs
through programming. Usually completed at renewal,
the requirement was intended to satisfy the public
interest standard. Formal ascertainment requirements
were relaxed during the deregulation period in the
1980s and 1990s.

Associational rights – These rights, which forbid the
government from preventing people from joining
organizations, are found implicitly in the First
Amendment guarantee to speak and assemble freely.
So long as the association or group in question does
not present a clear and present danger, or advocate
illegal activity, it is fully protected by the First
Amendment (unless subject to a "time, place and
manner" restriction). However, this right does not
always work both ways, as there are certain situations
where the government may force a group to include
members.

Authoritarian theory of the press – of all of the
press theories, authoritarian has been the most widely
used and is still the basis for many press systems --
particularly in Central and South America and third

world countries. Under the authoritarian system, the press is controlled (not owned) in function and operation by an organized society through the institution of government. It is controlled in order to prevent it from interfering with the goals of the state.

BBBBB

Berne Convention - an international copyright treaty, which the U.S joined in 1988. Applies international intellectual property restrictions to all member counties. The Universal Copyright Convention, 1955, is a similar agreement. Both are international agreements to respect copyright laws of member countries.

Bono Act – see Copyright Term Extension Act

Booth Rule - use of a person's name or likeness in advertising for a particular medium if the name or likeness has or will be used as a part of the medium's news or information content is not an appropriation, may be used in same medium or across media.

Brandenburg Test – test resulting from Brandenburg v. Ohio, which distinguishes between the advocacy of ideas and the incitement to unlawful conduct.

The four elements of the test are as follows:
1. Targeted speech must advocate the use of illegal force or violence
.2. Must be directed toward actually inciting such illegal conduct.
3. Must be imminent or immediate.

4. Must actually be likely to produce the illegal conduct.

Broadcast Decency Enforcement Act – signed into law in June 2006; increased penalties for indecency on broadcast television from $32,500 per violation to $325,000 per violation.

Broadcasting – transmission of radio or television signals intended for reception by the general public as distinguished from police/military point to point etc. and from cable broadcasting, which does not use the airwaves.

The following distinguishes between network tv, local tv, and cable:

Broadcast TV networks create and aggregate programming on a national basis, and affiliate with local broadcast TV stations to distribute that programming to viewers. These are networks like ABC, CBS, CW, Fox, MyTV, and NBC.

Local broadcast TV stations use the public airwaves to distribute that programming free over-the-air to households with TV antennas, and negotiate with local cable, satellite, and telephone companies to distribute that same programming to the distributors' customers. The local broadcast TV stations often create local news and other programming, and are typically known by their call letters or channel numbers, like NBC4 or Fox5.

A cable network creates and aggregates programming on a national basis, and negotiates with local and national distributors like cable companies, satellite companies, and telephone companies to distribute them to customers. They typically do not use the public airwaves.

CCCCC

Candidate Access Rule (Section 312) – requires that broadcasters provide access to candidates for federal office; does not cover local candidates but such denial might be determined inappropriate under the public interest standard.

Canon 35 – ABA rule preventing the use of cameras/taking of photographs in the courtroom; adopted as a result of disorder created by reporters and photographers during the trial of Bruno Hauptman in 1935. Canon 35 was later revised by the ABA to include video cameras and was renamed ABA 3A7.

CAN-SPAM [Controlling the Assault of Non-Solicited Pornography and Marketing Act], 2003 – regulation of Internet e-mail:

> 1.Prohibits use of false header information in commercial email
> 2.Requires unsolicited messages to include opt-out instructions
> 3.Protects against spam containing unmarked pornography

Central Hudson test – The Supreme Court devised this test in Central Hudson Gas & Elec. Corp. v. Public Service Commission of New York (1980) to determine when commercial speech would receive First Amendment protection. When deciding if the First Amendment should shield commercial speech, courts must consider whether:

1.The expression of commercial speech concerns lawful activity and is not misleading.
2.The asserted government interest is substantial.
3.The regulation directly advances the asserted government interest.
4.The regulation is no more extensive than necessary to serve that interest.

Certiorari (writ of certiorari) – Certiorari, meaning in Latin to "be more fully informed," is the procedure used by the Supreme Court and appellate courts to review the cases they hear. After receiving an appeal, the court decides whether to grant certiorari and review the lower court's case. If it grants certiorari, or "cert," then the higher court reviews the case. If the court denies cert, then the lower court ruling stands. In the Supreme Court, the votes of four justices are required to grant certiorari.

Change of venue / change of verniremen – compensatory remedies for prejudicial publicity; change of venue is when the trial is moved; change of veniremen is when the trial is kept in the same location, but the jury is chosen at a different location and imported daily to the trial site.

Child Online Protection Act [COPA] – (son of CDA) passed by Congress in 1998, intended to require identification for access to adult sites, was enjoined and has been ruled unconstitutional, by federal courts, upheld by USSC in Ashcroft v. ACLU, 2002, and again in Gonzalez v. ACLU, 2007.

Child pornography – material depicting children displayed in sexually explicit conduct; does not have to fulfill the requirements of obscenity to be outlawed under *New York v. Ferber*, 1982.

Child Pornography Prevention Act [CPPA] of 1996 – banned the sale and distribution [including internet] of materials which appear to depict minors performing sexually explicit acts . . . including computer/electronic generated images. [While the original was intended to prevent the exploitation of children, the rationale for including computer images was to protect children from pedophiles and child molesters who might be stimulated by such images.] *Ashcroft v. Free Speech Coalition*, 2002 – ruled invalid, child pornography must involve actual children / not virtual or computer generated children.

Children's Internet Protection Act [CIPA] – stipulates that public libraries cannot receive certain federal funds unless they install obscenity/child pornography blocking software on computers in public areas. Upheld in U.S. v. American Library Association, 2003. Ruling does require that libraries respond to any adults wishing to have the block removed for adult use.

Children's Television Act, 1990 – comprehensive FCC regulating television broadcast intended for audience composed largely of children:

1. limits number of minutes of advertising per hours in children's television to 10.5 on weekends and 12 on weekdays (before, during and after programming meant for children 12 years and older)
2. requires broadcasters to serve the educational needs of children including positive development (FCC stipulated three hours per week of educational programming for children up to 17)
3. outlaws program length commercials (when a product associated with the program is advertised in the program or attached at the end)
4. established safe harbor for broadcasting indecency now at 10 p.m. - 6 a.m.

Children's Online Privacy Protection Act, 1998 – allows FTC to regulate internet sites that collect personal information from children under 13.

Civil Contempt – punishment used to protect the rights of a private party in a legal dispute, i.e., a reporter refusing to divulge a source gets jail time 'til compliance.

Civil law – non-criminal law, involves individual private parties (companies, even government in limited cases) suing for some legal relief.

Clear and present danger – In *Schenck v. United States (1919),* Justice Oliver Wendell Holmes articulated this test, which said that the government may suppress speech that presents a clear and present danger, as long as the government can show that that danger is both real and imminent.

Collective works – an assortment of original, copyrighted or copyrightable pieces (i.e., a collection of original short stories) selected, edited etc. and copyrightable as a collection.

Commercial Speech Doctrine – protects legitimate advertising . . . fair and accurate advertising; protected under intermediate scrutiny – doesn't contribute to important political discussion . . . requires a substantial state interest for regulation.

Commercial Purpose – in privacy law commercial purpose involves advertising in television, radio, np, magazines, display of photos in studio, a false testimonial, a commercial feature film, situation comedy, or a novel, or in a banner ad or commercial message on the internet.

Common Law – Judge made law. Origins in England in the 12th and 13th Centuries when law was first developed. Disputes were initially settled according to custom (community custom), thus common throughout England or . . . common law (as distinguished from church law). Today, common law or case law is the custom of the court, based on precedent (what has happened in the past).

Communications Act of 1934 – re-established the 1927 law to cover all forms of communications (including telephone and telegraph); established the Federal Communications Commission (now 5 member/no more than 3 from one political party) to regulate communications.

Communication Decency Act [CDA] – included in the 1996 Telecommunications Act, directed at indecent materials on the internet, was found unconstitutional in Reno v. ACLU, 1997.

Compelled speech – As a general rule, the government cannot force an individual to express himself in a way that he would not otherwise do. This principle stems from *West Virginia State Board of Education v. Barnette* (1943), which held that a state could not force students to recite the Pledge of Allegiance. However, complications arise when commercial speech is involved, because companies, not people, are expressing themselves, and some advertising and other commercial speech can be regulated.

Compensatory Remedies – legal procedures intended to compensate for prejudicial publicity.

Pre-trial compensatory remedies include:
1. Voir dire - the questioning of potential jurors
2. Change of venue – moving trial to a new location
3. Change of veniremen – keeping trial in original location, but importing jury
4. Continuance – postponing trial until publicity dies down

Remedies applied during the trial:
1. Admonition – juror instructions; jury may be told not to discuss trial outside of the courtroom
2. Sequestration – jury is isolated from publicity about the trial

Compilation – a group of existing non-original, non-copyrightable materials (i.e., names in a telephone book); may be protected only if it requires some creativity in selecting and assembling, but not just because it was a lot of work.

Comstock Law, 1873 – one of the first regulations of obscenity; said that obscene books, pamphlets, pictures, etc. were non-mailable. Its weakness – it didn't define obscenity.

Constitutional Law - That which is written into the constitution and the amendments. Constitution is the Supreme Law of the Land.

Constitutional Amendment – an amendment to the United States Constitution requires a two-step process: proposal and ratification. A proposal may be made either by a vote of two-thirds of the members of both the House and Senate or at a convention called by two-thirds of the states; and ratified by three-fourths of the state legislatures or by three-fourths of ratifying conventions in the states. There have been 27 amendments to the constitution, including the original 10 in the Bill of Rights. The last amendment ratified was in 1992.

Confidential Source - a source who provides information to a reporter only when the source is guaranteed confidentiality (remain anonymous). It was ruled in Branzburg v. Hayes that reporters do not have privilege and may be required to identify a confidential source when it is determined to be in the best interest of society, i.e., when important to the defense or prosecution in a criminal trial.

Contempt Power – Judge's power to control what goes on inside his/her courtroom . . . punishable by a fine or time in jail. the extreme exercise of which is summary contempt power - the judge's power to accuse, find guilty and sentence in one blow of the gavel.

> 1. Civil contempt – punishment used to protect the rights of a private party in a legal dispute, i.e., a reporter refusing to divulge a source . . . is given jail time until he/she agrees to comply
> 2. Criminal contempt – punishment used to protect the law, authority of the court or power of the judge, i.e., reporter takes a photo after judge orders that no photos be taken, or reporter tries to talk to a juror. (Direct criminal contempt results from an act taking place inside the courtroom; Indirect criminal contempt results from an act taking place outside the courtroom)

Content neutral restrictions – speech/expression restrictions based on factors other than content . . . i.e., assembly in middle of a busy intersection, placement of news racks in front of a business door, distribution of pamphlets in a residential neighborhood at certain times. . . Restrictions require only intermediate scrutiny.

Continuance – compensatory remedy for prejudicial publicity in which the trial is postponed for a period of time until publicity dies down and a defendant may be more likely to receive a fair trial.

Controlling Remedies – legal procedures intended to control publicity about an ongoing trial

1.Restrictive (gag) orders – judge issue restrictions on ability of media to report certain information or what trial participants are allowed to say
2.Trial closure

COPA – See Child Online Protection Act

Copyright – body of law dealing with intangible property which exists to protect the original/intellectual creations [intellectual property] of authors, composers, artists, inventors, playwrights etc. Gives the creator of the original work the sole right to reproduce in any form and profit from his or her work. Gives creator economic incentive to create and thus benefit society. [Copyright can be transferred . . . given away, sold, leased or passed on to airs.]

The following are protected under copyright law:
1.Literary works (including software)
2.Musical works (including words)
3.Dramatic works (including music)
4.Pantomimes and choreographic works
5.Pictorial, graphic and sculptural works (Mickey Mouse)
6.Motion pictures and other audiovisual works
7.Sound recordings
8.Architectural works/drawings

Copyright law, constitutional basis – copyright law is authorized by Article I, Section 8, of the United States Constitution: *Congress shall have the power . . . to promote the progress of science and useful arts, by securing for limited times to authors and inventors the exclusive right to their respective writings and discoveries.*

Copyright, exclusive rights – under American copyright law, the holder of the copyright is granted specific and exclusive rights over his or her creations.

Following are exclusive rights held by the copyright owner:
1. Right to reproduce the copyrighted work
2. Right to make derivative works
3. Right to distribute the work publicly
4. Right to publicly perform a work
5. Right to publicly display a work
6. Right to transmit a sound recording, such as a CD, through digital audio means.

Copyright Notice – the word Copyright, Copr., ©, the year of publication, and the name of the copyright holder - Copyright © 2001 Joe Doakes; not required under agreements of the Berne Convention.

Copyright Term Extension Act, 1998 – also known as the Sonny Bono Copyright Term Extension Act or the Sony Bony Act; extends copyright protection by 20 years: life plus 70 for any and all new works; 95 years for works created prior to 1978; and for works for hire, 95 years from first publication or 120 years from creation.

Creative Commons – a nonprofit organization that enables the sharing and use of creativity and knowledge through free legal tools; free, easy-to-use copyright licenses provide a simple, standardized way to give the public permission to share and use your creative work — on conditions of your choice. CC licenses let you easily change your copyright terms from the default of "all rights reserved" to "some rights reserved." Creative Commons licenses are not an alternative to copyright. They work alongside copyright and enable you to modify your copyright terms to best suit your needs. (www.creative commons.org)

Following are the types of license available through Creative Commons:

Attribution – This license lets others distribute, remix, tweak, and build upon your work, even commercially, as long as they credit you for the original creation. This is the most accommodating of licenses offered. Recommended for maximum dissemination and use of licensed materials.

Attribution–Share-Alike – This license lets others remix, tweak, and build upon your work even for commercial purposes, as long as they credit you and license their new creations under the identical terms. This license is often compared to "copyleft" free and open source software licenses. All new works based on yours will carry the same license, so any derivatives will also allow commercial use. This is the license used by Wikipedia, and is recommended for materials that would benefit from incorporating content from Wikipedia and similarly licensed projects.

Attribution-No-Derivs – This license allows for redistribution, commercial and non-commercial, as long as it is passed along unchanged and in whole, with credit to you.

Attribution-Non-Commercial – This license lets others remix, tweak, and build upon your work non-commercially, and although their new works must also acknowledge you and be non-commercial, they don't have to license their derivative works on the same terms.

Attribution-Non-Commercial-Share-Alike – This license lets others remix, tweak, and build upon your work non-commercially, as long as they credit you and license their new creations under the identical terms.

Attribution-Non-Commercial-No-Derivs – This license is the most restrictive of our six main licenses, only allowing others to download your works and share them with others as long as they credit you, but they can't change them in any way or use them commercially.

Criminal Contempt – punishment used to protect law, authority of the court, or power of the judge, i.e. reporter takes photo after judge orders no photos, or reporter tries to talk with a juror. Direct = inside court (photo); indirect = outside (publishing info which has been gagged)

Criminal law – involves government prosecution of private individual on behalf of society; punishment usually fine or imprisonment (proof beyond a reasonable doubt required).

Critical Information Infrastructure Act – a part of the Homeland Security Act of 2002, which exempts from FOIA and local laws so-called critical infrastructure information that is voluntarily submitted to the federal government by private persons and business entities.

CTEA – Copyright Term Extension Act

Cyber libel – umbrella term referring to libel in cyberspace/online, including email, messaging or any of the various social media sites.

DDDDD

Defamation – that which causes damage/harm to a person's reputation – or exposes that person to hatred, contempt, ridicule; or that which:

   a. Damages one's reputation.
   b. Causes one's friends to avoid them.
   c. Deprives one of the ability to earn a living.

Defendant – in a civil case, person against whom suit is being filed; in a criminal case, the person being prosecuted.

Deontological – duty based; an approach to ethics that judges the morality of an action based on the action's adherence to a rule or rules. Sometimes described as "duty" or "obligation" or "rule" based ethics, because rules "bind you to your duty."

Derivative works - a work that is based on a preexisting work; copyrightable as a new work with the addition of sufficient originality. However, the original owner holds the right to create derivative works.

Dickinson Rule - contempt citation may stand even though a court order which resulted in the citation is later ruled invalid. (Not accepted in all jurisdictions).

Digital Millennium Copyright Act (1998) incorporates much of what was in the WIPO treaties.

> 1. Prohibits circumvention of technology which controls access to copyrighted material on the internet.
> 2. Outlaws manufacture of devices which are intended to circumvent controls.
> 3. Exempts internet service providers from copyright liability for transmitting materials others have put onto the internet.
> 4. Imposes a compulsory licensing/royalty scheme for the transmission of music on the internet.

EEEEE

Egalitarianism - a political philosophy that says all people should be treated as equals and have the same political, economic, social, and civil rights; basis of Rawl's veil of ignorance.

Electronic FOIA, 1996 - applies same rules as the original FOIA to electronic information. Includes same nine exemptions (see FOIA entry).

Electronic Communication Privacy Act of 1986 - comprehensive in protecting against hacking and interception of private e-mail, although it does not apply to employers.

Elements of Journalism - based on work by the Committee of Concerned Journalists distilled in a book by Bill Kovach and Tom Rosenstiel, "The Elements of Journalism: What Newspeople Should Know and the Public Should Expect," is a modern take on the Hutchins Commission recommendation in the mid-20th Century.

Recommendation of the group are as follows:

1.Journalism's first obligation is to the truth.
2.Its first loyalty is to citizens
3.Its essence is a discipline of verification.
4.Its practitioners must maintain an independence from those they cover.
5.It must serve as an independent monitor of power.
6.It must provide a forum for public criticism and compromise.
7.It must strive to make the significant interesting and relevant.
8.It must keep the news comprehensive and proportional.

9.Its practitioners must be allowed to exercise their personal conscience.

Equal Access Act, 1984 – forbids schools from discriminating against clubs, or denying them equal access to school facilities because of their philosophical or religious viewpoints. The act was largely passed to prevent widespread discrimination against religious clubs.

Equal Time/Opportunity Rule (Section 315) - if a broadcast station permits one legally qualified candidate for office use its facilities, it must give all candidates for the same office an equal opportunity. Stations may not censor political broadcasts and therefore may not be held accountable for the content of political.

Ethics – body of moral principles intended to guide human conduct. The study of ethics includes the following three branches:

1. **Metaethics** - examines the meaning of abstract terms such as good, right, justice, fairness etc.
2. **Normative ethics** - develops general theories, rules and principles of moral behavior. Aristotle is concerned with normative ethics in developing his Golden Mean.
3. **Applied ethics** - problem solving branch of ethics; uses principles of normative ethics to address specific ethical issues.

Ethical Conduct – conduct or behavior which is right or which conforms to the standards of a given society at a given time . . . conduct which is good out of a sense of moral conviction rather than from a fear of punishment.

Ethical mutualism – combining the deontological (duty based) view with the teleological (consequence-based) view. One might, for example, believe in the consistency of the categorical imperative, but allow for variance under exceptional circumstances or when the consequence merit.

Ethical principles – definitions of the following ethical principles may be found under the individual listings:

1. Aristotle's Golden Mean
2. Kant's Categorical Imperative (Deontological)
3. Utilitarianism (Teleological)
4. Rawl's Veil of Ignorance
5. Agape

Executive Law – Legal pronouncements by political executives. Elected officials from the U.S. president to mayors have limited powers to issue executive orders. (Bush II administration & signing statements)

Expert endorsements – advertising law requires that those endorsing products have appropriate expertise. Endorsers must actually use the product. Material connections between a product and the endorser must be disclosed. Endorsements by "typical consumers" must be made by real consumers, not actors.

Expectation of privacy – breaks down into public place vs. private place. In a public place, there is no expectation of privacy. Photos may be taken and voices recorded without one's knowledge (although some states have laws forbidding hidden cameras and recorders). Also, that which occurs on private property, but which is visible from the public areas is also considered beyond the zone of privacy. A zone of privacy likely does exist in your private residence, hospital room, ambulance, rented hotel room or private room in a restaurant.

FFFFF

Fair Comment – libel defense allowing defamatory opinion on matters of public concern. Matters of public concern: educational, religious, charitable, and professional organizations; manufacturers of products sold to the public; businesses serving the public (restaurants, theaters, etc.); any literary or artistic work; artists, writers, actors and actresses, athletes, coaches etc.

Fairness Doctrine – earlier doctrine under which broadcasters were required to devote reasonable time to broadcasting controversial issues/public issues; and coverage of controversial issues had to be balanced . . . both sides had to be presented and the broadcaster was responsible for finding a spokesperson for the other side or providing programming which aired the other side. Was repealed under the Reagan administration in 1986, but has been periodically reconsidered and proposed for reinstitution.

Fair Use - provision of copyright law (Section 107), which permits limited copying of protected materials for productive purposes such as criticism, comment, news reporting, teaching, and scholarship or research.

Section 107 stipulates that the following four factors be considered in determining fair use (reprinted from the federal copyright office website, copyright.gov):

1. Purpose and character of the use, including whether the use is of a commercial nature or is for nonprofit educational purposes: Courts look at how the party claiming fair use is using the copyrighted work, and are more likely to find that nonprofit educational and noncommercial uses are fair. This does not mean, however, that all nonprofit education and noncommercial uses are fair and all commercial uses are not fair; instead, courts will balance the purpose and character of the use against the other factors below. Additionally, "transformative" uses are more likely to be considered fair. Transformative uses are those that add something new, with a further purpose or different character, and do not substitute for the original use of the work.

2. Nature of the copyrighted work: This factor analyzes the degree to which the work that was used relates to copyright's purpose of encouraging creative expression. Thus, using a more creative or imaginative work (such as a novel, movie, or song) is less likely to support a claim of a fair use than using a factual work (such as a technical article or news item). In addition, use of an unpublished work is less likely to be considered fair.

3. Amount and substantiality of the portion used in relation to the copyrighted work as a whole: Under this factor, courts look at both the quantity and quality of the copyrighted material that was used. If the use includes a large portion of the copyrighted work, fair use is less likely to be found; if the use employs only a small amount of copyrighted material, fair use is more likely. That said, some courts have found use of an entire work to be fair under certain circumstances. And in other contexts, using even a small amount of a copyrighted work was determined not to be fair because the selection was an important part—or the "heart"—of the work.

4. Effect of the use upon the potential market for or value of the copyrighted work: Here, courts review whether, and to what extent, the unlicensed use harms the existing or future market for the copyright owner's original work. In assessing this factor, courts consider whether the use is hurting the current market for the original work (for example, by displacing sales of the original) and/or whether the use could cause substantial harm if it were to become widespread.

False Light – form of invasion of privacy; publication of false information. Similar to libel in that it deals with falsity, but does not have to be damaging, merely offensive. (This category is the one adopted by the least number of states.)

False/deceptive advertising – in order to be considered false or deceptive, an advertisement must contain the following:

> 1. There must be a representation, omission, or practice likely to mislead the consumer.
> 2. The act or practice must be considered from the perspective of a consumer who is acting reasonably under the circumstances (a reasonable member of the targeted group).
> 3. The representation, omission or practice must be material. (it's ok for example, to use perfectly formed plastic ice cubes in an ad for soft drinks, but not in an ad for ice cubes)

Federal Communications Commission – an administrative agency of the federal government created by the 1934 Communications Act. Its current mission is described as "regulat(ing) interstate and international communications by radio, television, wire, satellite and cable in all 50 states."

Federal Dilution Trademark Act, 1996 – protects trademark owners from use of the same or similar trademark even on dissimilar products. Previously, for example, someone could not have used the Walkman name on a portable CD player but could have used it on a treadmill or other machinery.

Federal Trade Commission – federal administrative agency created in 1914 with the self-described mission of "Working to protect consumers by preventing anticompetitive, deceptive, and unfair business practices, enhancing informed consumer choice and public understanding of the competitive process, and accomplishing this without unduly burdening legitimate business activity." Before taking action on a particular advertisement or advertising campaign, the FTC must establish that the ad in question is deceptive or untruthful, involves interstate commerce, and that the action proposed would actually be in the public interest.

FTC Remedies – the Federal Trade Commission has a variety of remedies it uses to combat potentially as well as proven false and/or misleading advertising. They include industry guidelines, voluntary orders, consent agreements, litigated orders, substantiation, corrective advertising, and injunctions.

Federal Sunshine Act, 1976 – federal open meetings law; applies to approximately 50 federal agencies, requiring that their meetings be conducted in public, that notices of meetings be give at least one week in advance, and that records be kept of closed meetings. Includes same nine exemptions as FOIA with the addition of a tenth exemption for meetings to discuss any legal arbitration involving the agency in question.

The exemptions are:
1. National Defense and foreign policy;
2. Internal personnel rules and practices
3. Statutory exemptions;
4. Proprietary information;
5. Accusation of crime or formal censure;

6. Personal privacy;
7. Investigatory records;
8. Financial institution reports;
9. Financial speculation and stability;
10. Issuance of subpoena, participation in civil action or proceeding, or formal agency adjudication.

Fighting Words – words that have a direct tendency to cause acts of violence by the person or persons to who the remark is made; doctrine enunciated in *Gooding v. Wilson*, 1972.

First Amendment – "Congress shall make no law respecting an establishment of religion, or prohibiting the free exercise thereof; or abridging the freedom of speech or of the press; or of the right of the people to peaceably assemble and to petition the government for a redress of grievances." Written by James Madison, the First Amendment was adopted by Congress in 1791 as one of the amendments contained in the Bill of Rights. It was originally proposed as the third amendment, but advanced to the number one position when amendments relating to apportionment and congressional pay were removed from the original list of amendments.

Flag Protection Act – adopted by Congress in 1989, intended to counter the ruling in *Texas v. Johnson* that flag burning was a protected form of expression. The Flag Protection Act was ruled invalid in *U.S. v. Eichman/U.S. v. Haggerty*. Said flag burning is an act of free expression protected by the First Amendment.

FOIA - Freedom of Information Act

Fourth Amendment – "The right of the people to be secure in their persons, houses, papers, and effects, against unreasonable searches and seizures, shall not be violated, and no Warrants shall issue, but upon probable cause, supported by Oath or affirmation, and particularly describing the place to be searched, and the persons or things to be seized."

Fourteenth Amendment – No state . . . shall deprive any person of life, liberty (including free expression) or due process of law. Interpreted in *Gitlow v. NY* in 1925 as protecting free expression from infringement by state & city governments. Section 1 of the amendment is reprinted below. The complete text is reprinted later in this guide as a part of the complete Constitutions and Amendments.

> **Section 1**: All persons born or naturalized in the United States and subject to the jurisdiction thereof, are citizens of the United States and of the State wherein they reside. No State shall make or enforce any law which shall abridge the privileges or immunities of citizens of the United States; nor shall any State deprive any person of life, liberty, or property, without due process of law; nor deny to any person within its jurisdiction the equal protection of the laws.

Four Theories of the Press – based on a 1956 book by Siebert, Peterson and Schramm. Brief definitions are given in the alphabetized listings:

> 1. Authoritarian theory

2. Soviet-Communist theory
3. Libertarian theory
4. Social responsibility theory

Freedom of Information Act, 1966 – federal law providing access to all records held by federal agencies (except Congress and federal courts) with nine exemptions.

1. National security matters
2. Housekeeping - internal personnel rules and practices
3. Material exempted by statute, i.e. Nuclear Regulatory etc.
4. Trade secrets and financial information (SBA applications etc.)
5. Interagency memo and pre-decisional working drafts
6. Personnel and medical files, the disclosure of which would constitute an invasion of privacy
7. Law enforcement records can be exempted if:
    a. interferes with law enforcement
    b. would deprive a person of the right to a fair trial
    c. would constitute an unwarranted invasion of privacy
    d. identifies a confidential source
    e. discloses enforcement techniques/procedures
    f. endangers the life or safety of an individual
8. Financial records relative to banking/financial institutions
9. Geological and geophysical data (re maps, wells etc.)

Free Flow of Information Act – a proposed federal shield law . . . under certain conditions would protect reporters from having to reveal confidential sources; first introduced in 2007, never passed.

FTC – Federal Trade Commission

FTC Endorsement Guides – Federal Trade Commission requirements between brands and endorsers when there is a material or financial relationship between the two. Following are the four basic guidelines for endorsements. See https://www.ftc.gov/news-events/blogs/business-blog/2017/09/three-ftc-actions-interest-influencers for additional information.

1. Clearly disclose when you have a financial or family relationship with a brand.
2. Don't assume that using a platform's disclosure tool is sufficient.
3. Avoid ambiguous disclosures like #thanks, #collab, #sp, #spon, or #ambassador.
4. Don't rely on a disclosure placed after a CLICK MORE link or in another easy-to-miss location.

Functions of the First Amendment – theories relative to the purpose or reason to be of the First Amendment:

1. Discovery of Truth / Marketplace of Ideas Theory – Milton; it is important for all speech to be allowed in the marketplace regardless of its content . . . ultimate good is reached through free trade of ideas; a rational people will be able to separate the truth from fiction, that truth will rise to the top.

2. Participation in Democracy /Access Theory – Media are public utilities; everyone should have access, thus leveling the playing field. Enunciated in mid-20th century without much reception on the part of media. Trend continued toward consolidation and conglomeration, thus allowing fewer voices in the marketplace.

3. Check on Government - the watchdog or fourth estate role . . . i.e. Watergate, Iraq prisoners, Walter Reed etc.

4. Self-realization, self-fulfillment theory – free expression can be important in that it allows a person or persons to express themselves, to establish identity and self-definition.

5. Safety-valve/social stability theory – allows individuals to blow off steam, without that right might explode.

GGGGG

Good Samaritan Provision (Section 230) – a provision of the Telecommunications Act of 1996 that provides immunity to internet service providers (site hosts) from responsibility for material posted on sites they control. Clarifies a distinction between traditional publishers and internet service providers. Prior to 1996, ISPs that monitored their sites to control content were considered "publishers" and thus responsible for content.

Group Identification – defamatory comment about a large group of more than 25-50 (courts vary) generally is not viewed as constituting libel against an individual member of the group. However, individual members of small groups may be defamed by blanket statements or slurs. For example, a potentially libelous remark about "New York cops" is not likely to be seen as defaming an individual member of the NYC police force, while a similar remark about a small police force in North Carolina might be actionable.

HHHHH

Hauptman trial - 1935 trial of Bruno Hauptman, accused and convicted of kidnapping and murdering Charles Lindbergh's 20-month old son. Lindbergh was known for making the first solo trans-Atlantic flight between New York and Paris. The trial's sensational press coverage led the American Bar Association to eventually put into place its Canon 35 (later to become ABA 3A7) to prevent cameras from being allowed inside courtrooms.

Hate crime – A criminal act committed out of hatred for a certain type or types of people. Hate crime laws generally allow states and federal prosecutors to impose heftier penalties against perpetrators of crime motivated by hatred based on characteristics such as race, religion, ethnicity, nationality, gender, sexual orientation, gender identity, and disability.

Heckler's veto – A heckler's veto occurs when government attempts to suppress speech (usually of an inflammatory nature) in order to avoid an undesirable reaction. Such suppression is generally a violation of the First Amendment per a 1949 Supreme Court decision in *Terminiello v. Chicago*.

Hicklin Rule – borrowed from the British, first widely used definition of obscenity, first used by the courts in the late 1800s: A work is obscene if it has a tendency to deprave and corrupt those whose minds are open to such immoral influences and into whose hands it might fall . . . if a part of the work is obscene then the whole work is obscene.

Homeland Security Act of 2002 – response to 9/11 terrorist attacks; created the department of Homeland Security, reorganizing several government agencies under one director.

IIIII

Identification – a requirement for proving libel, one may be identified by name, photo, pen name, nickname, initials, pen/ink drawing, circumstance, putting two stories together. (Note that misidentification is determined by audience perception. While you may have a person in mind, if the audience perceives the information to be about someone else, then that someone else is identified. . . making it important to accurately identify people).

Incidental Use – walking through the scene or background of a movie, insignificant uses of an individual's name, being a part of a large group; not considered appropriation.

Incitement standard, incitement to violence – Test for determining if certain types of speech can be restricted. Based on decision in *Brandenburg v. Ohio*, 1969

> Says that the targeted speech must be:
> 1. directed at inciting or producing imminent lawless action
> 2. likely to produce or incite such action.

Indecency – "Indecent" speech usually receives First Amendment protection, except when it is broadcast over the airwaves. In *FCC v. Pacifica* (1978), the Supreme Court held that the Federal Communications Commission could regulate indecent speech because broadcast media are both uniquely pervasive and uniquely accessible to children.

For regulatory purposes, the FCC defines indecency as *"language or material that, in context, depicts or describes, in terms patently offensive as measured by contemporary community standards for the broadcast medium, sexual or excretory activities or organs."* The term "indecent material" is simply material that may be sexually graphic and may be limited to adults only, but is not outside of First Amendment protection.

Influencer, influencer marketing – the digital age's version of celebrity advertising in which anyone with a significant following on social media (including traditional celebrities as well as internet made "influencers") are paid to market products and services. As a result of the popularity of influencer marketing on sites such as Instagram and You Tube, the Federal Communications Commission has become actively engaged in regulating the brand relationship with influencers. Like traditional endorsers in advertising, social media influencers are required to follow FTC Endorsement Guides when there is a material relationship between the brand and endorser.

Innocent construction rule – if it is possible to interpret a statement in an innocent or non-damaging way then no libel has occurred.

Intentional Infliction of Emotional Distress – tort involving outrageous conduct intended to cause severe emotional damage to another. Was an issue in the *Hustler v. Falwell* case. Requires that:

1. Defendant's conduct is intentional or reckless
2. Defendant's conduct is extreme and outrageous
3. Defendant's caused plaintiff emotional distress
4. The emotional distress was severe

Intrusion - determined by "reasonable expectation of privacy"; if the court feels the plaintiff had a reasonable expectation of privacy at the time a photo is snapped or a voice is recorded then the plaintiff will win.

Invasion of Privacy – see "Privacy"

JJJJJ

John Milton – 17th century English writer/poet/scholar; while perhaps best known for his epic poem *Paradise Lost,* he also is recognized for his defense of a free press in an important speech titled "Areopagitica."

Judicial Activism – judges who create rights (enact legislation) not explicitly stated in the constitution or overturn laws based on their feelings that a statute is unfair or bad policy. Based on personal and political beliefs rather than existing laws.

Judicial Restraint – the belief that a judge's role is not to make policy but to interpret the law as written in the constitution or passed by congress or the states. (Also called strict constructionism.)

Judicial Review – the right of any court to declare any law or official governmental action to be invalid because it violates the constitution (*Marbury v. Madison*, 1803).

Judicial System – the American system of courts include both state and federal courts, which interpret and apply the laws of a particular jurisdiction. Both have trial courts and appellate courts:

> **Trial Courts** – fact finding courts, where most cases begin, juries.

> **Appellate Courts** – law reviewing courts, consider whether or not the law has been properly applied in light of the facts.

State courts are generally divided into the following:

1. Trial courts of limited jurisdiction (traffic)

2. Trial courts of general jurisdiction (county)
3. Court of Appeals - intermediary
4. State Supreme Court

Federal Courts include the following:

1. U.S. District Courts (94, every state has at least one)
2. U.S. Court of Appeals (13 including 12 circuits) *(13th is nationwide, hearing appeals in specific kinds of cases, i.e., patent cases)*
3. U.S. Supreme Court – *decision binding on lower courts*

Jurisdiction – power to enforce laws . . . may be territorial or subject-matter related . . . i.e. broadcast, cable, copyright, patents, access issues are under federal jurisdiction; privacy, reputation, zoning, unfair competition, access to state & local government are under state jurisdiction; trademarks, corporate speech, advertising, antitrust and obscenity may be under both state and federal jurisdictions.

KKKKK

Kant's Categorical Imperative – philosophical principle, which says one should "Act on that maxim which you will to become a universal law" . . . or make a decision in a manner you wish similar situations to be decided. Kant's view is an absolute, unconditional duty based rule. There are no exceptions. Lying is wrong . . . always wrong. Would still be wrong if you can save someone from dying by lying. And, if lying is wrong, deception to get a story is inexcusable.

This is called a deontological (duty based) view, meaning it is a moral obligation to act in a certain way and must be obeyed regardless of the consequences.

LLLLL

Lanham Act – trademark protection law; applies also to false advertising: "Any person who in commercial advertising or promotion, misrepresents the nature, characteristics, qualities, or geographic origin of his or her or another person's goods, services, or commercial activities, shall be liable in a civil action by any person who believes that he or she is or is likely to be damaged by such act."

Law – Set of rules which attempt to guide human conduct and a set of sanctions which are applied when those rules are violated. The sanction or punishment for violating law distinguishes law from ethics. Some sources of law are:

1. Common Law or Case Law - law that is based on custom or precedent.

2. Statutory Law - legislative or written law; laws created by elected bodies from city councils to state legislatures, to the federal Congress

3. Constitutional Law - law based on the U.S. Constitution; the supreme law of the land

4. Administrative Law - quasi law or guidelines created by federal agencies such as the Federal Communications Commission, the Federal Trade Commission etc. The Commissions are created by a legal act of Congress to administer the policy of the agency.

5. Executive Law - policy generated within the power of the chief administrators of government.

Law of Equity – system of law developed in England for the purpose of granting solutions based on what was fair; used where common law (law custom) could not provide a solution. Applies solutions other than money damages.

Levels of Scrutiny – the USSC considers the following three levels of scrutiny when deciding First Amendment cases:

1. Minimum Scrutiny – government action to restrict speech/press is valid if it involves any legitimate government interest that is not overbroad . . . most all unprotected speech falls into this category (obscenity, false/misleading commercial advertising, fighting words, libel with fault, threats to national security, sexual harassment). These considered low-value speech/not necessary to a democratic society.

2. Intermediate Scrutiny – government action is valid if narrowly drawn to advance a substantial state interest . . . protected with limits (truthful commercial advertising . . . doesn't contribute to important social discourse, and lottery advertising for example.) Also, applied to most all content neutral TPM (time, place, manner) restrictions . . . posters on telephone poles, time limits on residential solicitation, signs impeding clear view etc. Expressive conduct cases[i.e. nude dancing] also may sometimes be decided under intermediate scrutiny.

3. Strict Scrutiny – government action is constitutional only if narrowly drawn to advance a compelling government interest. Fully protected speech (political speech, expressive content based speech. (Cohen v. California, 1971, case . . . re "fuck the draft" on back of coat worn into LA County Courthouse . . . Cohen convicted under California law, which prohibits disturbing the peace by offensive conduct. Court ruled protected speech absent a compelling reason to prevent.

Libel – printed defamation as opposed to slander which is spoken (Virtually all media defamation is tried as libel) . . . also a false allegation of fact that is disseminated about a person and that tends to injure that person's reputation. Requirements for proving libel: Publication, Identification, Defamation, Falsity and Fault.

Libel Damages – Actual, special, presumed, and punitive.

Libel Defenses –Statute of limitations, privilege, rhetorical hyperbole, fair comment, right of reply, retraction, wire service defense, neutral reporting and libel-proof plaintiff.

Libel per se – libel on its face (thief, burglar, embezzlers).

Libel per quod – innocent on its face, but libelous when considered with other facts: To say someone is pregnant ok, 'cept when considered with the fact that the husband is and has been overseas for past 10 months.

Libel-proof plaintiff – libel defense; when a plaintiff's reputation is so bad additional false accusations could not be shown to be damaging.

Libertarian theory of the press – developed in 17th - 18th century England. It was believed that: Man is a rational being and is capable of making decisions to advance his own interests. Society or state exists to allow man to accomplish his objectives. Relative to intellectual pursuit, man is rational and thus capable of discovering truth on his own.

Milton, Areopagitica, 1644, wrote: "Man is rational, can distinguish right from wrong, good and bad, should have unlimited access to the ideas and thoughts of other men," resulting in the open marketplace of ideas . . . in which everyone is allowed to speak as it is believed that the truth will rise to the top . . . the self-righting process ... even if falsity gains temporary victory, truth will eventually win out.

License Renewal – Broadcast licenses are renewed every 8 years. Generally, it currently is a near automatic process (renewal expectancy to renewal near-certainty). Under the Telecommunications Act of 1996, an incumbent (current license holder) is renewed as long as:

1. the station has served the public interest, convenience and necessity
2. there have been no serious violations of FCC rules, and
3. there has been no pattern of abuse

Limited public figure – in libel law a normally private person who has voluntarily placed himself into the middle of a public controversy with the intent to have an impact on the resolution of that controversy; such an individual would be required to prove actual malice in a libel suit.

MMMMM

Memorandum Order – an opinion of the court publishing the vote without a written opinion.

Meiklejohnian Theory – Meiklejohn theroizes that there are two types of speech

1. Speech related to the self-governing process - receives absolute protection [maximum scrutiny]

2. Speech not related to self-governing process - balanced with other rights. [minimum/intermediate scrutiny]

Minnesota Gag Law – allowed courts to declare any obscene, lewd, lascivious, malicious or defamatory publication a public nuisance and stop publication. Ruled unconstitutional in *Near v. Minnesota*, 1931.

Misappropriation/unfair competition - largely common law which prevents one from either trying to pass off his/her work as the work of someone else, or trying to pass off the work of someone else as their own. A radio station which reads its news from a local newspaper, thus gaining an unfair advantage, would be guilty of misappropriation and unfair competition.

Moral Rights – protects a work's integrity and reputation of the creator regardless of who purchases; can't use or change a work in a way that would reflect negatively on the creator's reputation [in U.S. law and Berne Convention agreement]. Limited and does not apply to works for hire. (Visual Artists Rights Act)

Multiple Ownership Rules – FCC mandated rules on broadcast ownership:

> 1. No limit on the number of radio stations that may be owned nationally

> 2. No limit on the number of TV stations that may be owned nationally . . . 39% of U.S. television households

> 3.Ownership limits within a single market based on size of market; larger the market the more stations may be owned by a single entity.

Must-carry rules — Sections 4 and 5 of the Cable Television Consumer Protection and Competition Act of 1992 forced cable operators to carry on their cable systems local commercial and public broadcast stations. In *Turner Broadcasting System v. FCC* (1997), the Supreme Court said these rules did not violate cable carriers' First Amendment rights because they were economic regulations aimed at preserving the viability of the local broadcast networks and because they were imposed on all cable systems without reference to the content offered.

NNNNN

Neutral reporting – protected in reporting accusation about a public figure from a reputable source even if suspect story is false; news is in the fact that the accusation is being made.

Net Neutrality – controversial doctrine stipulating that the internet's broadband providers (Spectrum, AT&T, Comcast, Cox etc.) should be regulated in such a manner that all websites receive equal treatment at the same rates, essentially like a utility. In 2017 the FCC controlled by the Trump administration moved to do away with rules regulating the internet, thus allowing the broadband providers to distinguish between content providers in terms of speed of delivery as well as cost.

Ninth Amendment – The enumeration in the Constitution of certain rights shall not be construed to deny or disparage others retained by the people.

(Sometimes referred to as one of the roots of privacy rights)

Non-originalist – one who is a proponent of a more flexible and alternative interpretation of constitution, allowing for changes in society and promoting the public good.

OOOOO

Obscenity – legal definition established in *Miller v. California*, 1973; remains the current definition of obscenity:

> 1. An average person, applying contemporary local [not national] community standards, finds that the work, taken as a whole appeals to prurient interest.

> 2. The work depicts in a patently offensive way sexual conduct specifically defined by state law.

> 3. The work in question lacks serious literary, artistic, political, or scientific value.

Open Marketplace of ideas – belief that the truth is best served by allowing everyone to speak; that when everyone is allowed to speak the truth will rise to the top . . . the self-righting process ... even if falsity gains temporary victory, truth will eventually win out. Espoused by Milton in Areopagitica.

Originalist – constitution means the same thing today as it did when it was drafted in 1787, making no allowances for societal change. Proponents may come at the view as either

1. textualists, those who look only at the words as they were written, and

2. intentionalists, those who attempt to interpret the intent of the founding fathers' words. Justice Scalia was both an originalist and a textualist.

Originality - copyright law protects only original creations or those, which owe their origin to the creator. A transcript of a trial cannot be copyrighted, for example, because it has no original element; a Christmas parade cannot by copyrighted because it is a common idea; raw footage can be copyrighted because there is originality in its shooting.

Original Jurisdiction – the first court to hear. The USSC is normally an appellate court with original jurisdiction in limited cases, such as in the event of a legal dispute between two states.

Orphan Work - a copyrighted work for which it is difficult or impossible, after reasonable effort, to discover and locate the owner. May result due to out-of-date information, death of an author, or non-registration. Copyrighted works are not required to be registered with the copyright office (creative works are protected on creation) and a notice of copyright ownership is no longer required.

PPPPP

Patent law – as opposed to copyright, patents protect utilitarian type items; includes protection for three different kinds of items:

> 1. Items which have utility such as a machine or process (typewriter or a way of reducing noise on an audiotape).
> 2. Design of an item, a piece of furniture for example.
> 3. Plants which are reproduced by cutting & grafting.

Patently Offensive – re the Miller v. California definition of obscenity; many states use Rehnquist's words: representation or description of the ultimate sex act, normal or perverted, actual or simulated; representation or description of masturbation, excretory functions, and lewd exhibition of the genitals.

Patriot Act – officially the USA Patriot Act (Uniting and Strengthening America by Providing Appropriate Tools Required to Intercept & Obstruct Terrorism Act of 2001).

> 1. expanded authority of FBI to issue National Security Letters requiring businesses to turn over customer records (and not tell customer)
> 2. sharing of grand jury information
> 3. sharing of contents of wire, oral and electronic communications obtained by law enforcement
> 4. access to stored voice mail

5. expanded power to access electronic communications
6. greater authority to trace internet communications
7. greater power re search warrants
8. Reapproved in 2006 with rewrites/civil liberty safeguards

Per Curiam decision – unsigned opinion representing an opinion of the court as a whole.

Personal Attack Rule – earlier rule that was a part of the Fairness Doctrine; stipulated that when a person was attacked editorially on the air during the discussion of a controversial issue of public importance, within one week, person attacked had to be:

1. be notified of the date, time, ID of the broadcast
2. be provided with a script, tape or summary of the broadcast
3. be given the opportunity to respond
The personal attack rule did not apply to political candidates or to news coverage including commentary. Repealed in 2000.

PICON Rule – stands for public interest, convenience and necessity; basis on which FCC is to regulate broadcasting; originated in the Federal Radio act of 1927

Plagiarism – the act of taking ideas, thoughts, or words from someone and using them/passing them off as your own.

Plaintiff – person bringing the suit, seeking some sort of relief or compensation.

Plaintiff's Case in libel suit - in order to win a libel case, the plaintiff must successfully show:

1. publication,
2. identification
3. defamation
4. falsity
5. fault, and
6. harm.

Plurality Decision – in an appellate decision, an opinion expressing the view of more judges than any other opinion, but less than a majority.

Political Editorials Rule – earlier rule that was a part of the Fairness Doctrine; stipulated that if station endorsed/opposed a political candidate, it had to within 24 hours provide the person attacked or not endorsed:

1. time, date, and ID of the broadcast
2. tape or summary of broadcast
3. opportunity to respond

The Political Editorials Rule was repealed in 2000.

Pornography – broad term used to describe sexually explicit materials, may or may not be obscene.

Potter Box – a system for considering situations and making reasoned ethical decisions. Without an organized approach to moral reasoning, we're merely making knee-jerk decisions on important issues. Developed by a Harvard professor of divinity. It does not give an answer, just a way of deciding. Includes four steps prior to the decision:

1. definition or analysis of the situation
2. consideration of values (that which is desirable) related to the decision
3. analysis of philosophical principles that could be used in making a reasoned decision (Golden Mean, Categorical Imperative, Utilitarianism, Veil of Ignorance, Agape); and
4. consideration of the various loyalties involved in the decision.

Preferred Position Balancing Theory – in balancing free expression with other rights, it is assumed that any limitation on speech or press is illegal. Free speech will be preferred; and other party must justify an infringement. Based on belief that the maintenance of all rights is based on freedom of speech and press.

Prejudicial publicity – information that has the potential of affecting a defendant's right to a fair trial (Sixth Amendment). The American Bar Association considers the following prejudicial:

1. Confessions
2. Lie detector results
3. Stories on defendant's past criminal record
4. Stories questioning the credibility of witnesses
5. Stories about a defendant's character
6. Stories which tend to inflame the public mood against the defendant.

7. Stories that suggest or declare that defendant is guilty

Prejudicial publicity, remedies for – remedies may be either compensatory or controlling. Compensatory remedies include voir dire, change of venue or change of veniremen, continuance, admonition, or sequestration. Controlling remedies include restrictive orders and trial closure.

Presumed Damages – damages which are awarded without proof of harm; public or private person suing for libelous statements involving matters of public concern must show actual malice.

Prior Restraint – the act of restraining or preventing publication. Most believe that if nothing else the First Amendment meant freedom from prior restraint.

Privacy – The right to be left alone; the right of individuals to control information about themselves; involves one of four separate offenses. The four should be thought of individually as potential problems.

1. Appropriation of name or likeness for commercial purposes without consent.
2. Publication of private/embarrassing information.
3. Intrusion into one's solitude.
4. Publication of false information/false light.

Privacy, Constitutional Roots of - the following are generally considered to be the constitutional roots of privacy:

1. First Amendment - protects privacy by ensuring protection from compelled disclosure. (Right to speak includes the right not to speak).

2. Fourth Amendment - protects citizens from unreasonable searches and seizures by government officials, protects privacy in one's home.

3. Ninth Amendment - ensures that the people have more rights than those listed in the Constitution; has been interpreted as including privacy protections.

4. Fourteenth Amendment - courts have interpreted the word "liberty" in the 14th Amendment's due process clause as encompassing protection for personal privacy.

Privilege – defense of libel stipulating that a person cannot be held responsible for comments made in a public forum. It extends to congressmen, senators, state representatives, city and county board members etc. . . . and to comments in a courtroom or grand jury room by judges, lawyers, witnesses etc. in relation to official proceedings. Media have a conditional or qualified privilege to report privileged conversations. (privilege applies to the protected conversation only, and it must be a fair and accurate report of the communications).

Promissory estoppel – law intended to prevent an injustice when someone fails to keep a promise . . . a promise on which someone has relied. Applied in *Cowles v. Cohen.*

1. defendant made a definite promise
2. defendant intended the promise and the plaintiff relied on the promise
3. upholding of the promise is required to prevent an injustice

Protect Act, 2003 – [Prosecutorial Remedies and Other Tools to End the Exploitation of Children Today Act] – replaces COPA, makes it illegal to send or receive an image that is indistinguishable from that of a minor in a sexual situation.

Public Forum – levels of free expression allowed may be determined by the type of forum in which the speech is exercised.

1. Traditional public forum – street corners, public parks (although can interfere with other people's rights, i.e., passing out pamphlets in front of post office); compelling state interest or strict scrutiny would be required to justify restrictions.

2. (Limited) Designated public forum – sometimes are and sometimes aren't public forum: school facilities outside of school hours, state fairgrounds, public airports, statehouse grounds, license plates, (i.e. S.C. plate with cross). Content based restrictions require compelling interest/strict scrutiny. Concept of neutrality applies when designated a public forum/gov. cannot discriminate re viewpoint. Military recruiters and peace activists have same right.

3. Public property not public forum – jails, military bases, telephone poles, mail boxes, airport terminals. Minimum scrutiny.

4. Private property as public forum – unclear though some interpretations suggest that where a mall, for example, takes on all the attributes of a public square it becomes a public forum

Public Official - for purposes of a libel suit a public official is someone who is usually elected to public office, controls a budget, and oversees employees. It is an important distinction because a public official suing for libel is required to prove actual malice: knowledge of falsity or reckless disregard for the truth.

Punitive Damages – damages awarded to punish the defendant; public or private person suing for libelous statements involving matters of public concern must show actual malice.

Publication in libel law – as defined by libel law, anything that is seen by a third person (personal letter from me to you about a third person is considered published). Includes anything published in a magazine, newspaper, aired on radio or television or appearing in a blog, tweet, or text message shared with a third person. Publication as defined by law of privacy requires exposure to a mass audience.

Publication in privacy law – exposure to a mass audience.

QQQQQ

Qualified immunity – A doctrine that protects government officials from liability in civil rights actions when they do not violate clearly established principles of law.

RRRRR

Radio Act of 1912 - required that all radio transmitters be licensed, and delegated the Secretary of Labor to assign wavelengths, set hours of operation etc. . . . be he/she could not refuse a request for a license. Anyone who applied could get a license to broadcast.

Radio Act of 1927 - regulated the technical aspects of broadcasting and the programming, licensing and renewal of licenses; established the Federal Radio Commission; and originated the rule on which all regulation is still based: Broadcasters must operate in the "public interest, convenience and necessity" (PICON Rule) at all times. Based on the belief that the airwaves belong to the public and that broadcasters who are allowed to use them should operate in the public interest.

Rawl's Veil of Ignorance - justice emerges when negotiating without social distinctions. Rawl's philosophy advocates that as we negotiate social disagreements, we do so from behind a veil where we are equal in the purest sense -- sex, race, class etc. without knowing where we fit when we come out from behind the veil . . . a sort of egalitarianism where all persons should be treated equally in terms of rights and opportunities.

Reardon Report (Standards Relating to Fair Trial and Free Press) – report following the Sheppard case in which it was recommended that in order to ensure defendants in a sensational trial a fair hearing

1. lawyers and judges involved in the trial should not talk to the media, and
2. judges should use their restrictive powers and contempt citations against those who violate the restrictive orders.

Reckless disregard — In *New York Times Co. v. Sullivan* (1964), the Supreme Court defined actual malice as a state of mind in which a person or publication makes an untrue and defamatory statement about a person "with knowledge that it was false or with reckless disregard of whether it was false or not." In order to recover damages for libel or defamation, a public official or public figure must be able to show by clear and convincing evidence that the defendant acted with actual malice.

Reporters' privilege — Reporters are protected, on a state-by-state basis, by statutory law or constitution, from testifying about confidential information or sources at trial. Reporters often use confidential sources for information that otherwise they would not be able to obtain. For a variety of reasons, the government (or others) may want the reporter to reveal her source. In many jurisdictions, but not all, the courts presume that the reporter has a right not to identify her confidential sources. Generally, the privilege will apply unless those trying to get the reporter to divulge her source make a case that:

1.Their claim has merit.
2.The information sought is necessary or critical to making their case.
3. A reasonable effort to acquire the information has not yielded any results.
4.The interest of the reporter in keeping the information secret is not supported by a need to preserve the confidentiality of the information.

Reporters on private property – contrary to what many believe, reporters do not have free access to enter private property even when covering a news event; officials do not have authority to invite reporters onto private property; consent must be given by the owner or owner's representative.

Re-publication – every republication of a libel is a new libel. Newspaper A reports that the Mayor of Burlington was arrested for soliciting a prostitute. Radio station B reports the story – even attributes the information to Newspaper A. Both the newspaper and the radio station can be sued. Exception: Those who distribute or sell the product not responsible – news vendors, book sellers, local TV stations transmitting network reports.

Restrictive (Gag) Orders – measures used by a court to protect a defendant's right to a fair trial; usually involves either gagging media directly or restricting what trial participants are allowed to say.

Retraction – timely publication of a correction of a libelous publication may reduce potential damage awards in many states.

Rhetorical Hyperbole – exaggeration or exaggerated statements of opinion; unbelievable rhetoric which no one would believe to be an assertion of fact.

Right of privacy – the right of an individual to not be embarrassed or humiliated or simply taken advantage of by having his/her name or likeness appropriated.

Right of publicity – right of celebrities to control the commercial exploitation of their name or likeness; the right to profit from one's own celebrity status. Right of publicity is a property right and may be passed on to heirs.

Right to gather information vs. right to disseminate – while the right to disseminate information is almost unlimited (*Cox v. Cohn*), there are significant limits on the information gathering process (*Zemel v. Rush, Houchins v. KQED, Wilson v Layne* etc.)

Right-of-reply – offering the target of a potentially damaging statement the opportunity to respond before published; may contribute positively to the defense.

SSSSS

Satire/parody - satire is a type of social criticism in which an individual is ridiculed for their vices or shortcomings; parody is a humorous or satirical imitation of art, music or literature for the purpose of commentary. Satire and parody are normally protected from charges of libel under fair comment defense. Parody is also protected from copyright infringement charges under fair use.

SCOTUS – Supreme Court of the United States

Scrutiny levels – standards of judicial review applied by the federal courts.

1. Minimum Scrutiny – government action to restrict speech/press is valid if it involves any legitimate government interest that is not overbroad . . . most all unprotected speech falls into this category (obscenity, false/misleading commercial advertising, fighting words, libel with fault, threats to national security, sexual harassment). These considered low-value speech/not necessary to a democratic society.

2. Intermediate Scrutiny – government action is valid if narrowly drawn to advance a substantial state interest . . . protected with limits (truthful commercial advertising . . . doesn't contribute to important social discourse, and lottery advertising for example.) Also, applied to most all content neutral TPM (time, place, manner) restrictions . . . posters on telephone poles, time limits on residential solicitation, signs impeding clear view etc. Expressive conduct cases [i.e. nude dancing] also may sometimes be decided under intermediate scrutiny.

3. Strict Scrutiny – government action is constitutional only if narrowly drawn to advance a compelling government interest. Fully protected speech (political speech, expressive content based speech. (*Cohen v. California*, 1971, case . . . re "fuck the draft" on back of coat worn into LA County Courthouse . . . Cohen convicted under California law, which prohibits disturbing the peace by offensive conduct. Court ruled protected speech absent a compelling reason to prevent.

Secondary effects — This doctrine, which arose out of adult-business zoning cases, provides that government officials have greater leeway to regulate adult businesses if they are concerned with the harmful side effects allegedly associated with these businesses — such as increased crime and decreased property values. However, especially at the local level, this doctrine has been applied outside of the adult-business context. According to many First Amendment advocates, the doctrine thus threatens to undermine existing First Amendment free-speech jurisprudence.

Sedition Act of 1918 – made it a crime to attempt to obstruct recruiting; to utter or print or write or publish disloyal or profane language that was intended to cause contempt of, or scorn for, the federal government, the constitution, the flag or the uniform of the armed services.

Sequestration – a compensatory remedy intended to prevent jurors from being exposed to prejudicial publicity by isolating the jury during the course of the trial, usually in a hotel.

Smith Act, 1940 – made it a crime to advocate violent overthrow of the government, to conspire to advocate the violent overthrow of the government, to organize a group that advocates the violent overthrow of the government, or to be a member of a group that advocates the violent overthrow of the government.

Single Mistake Rule – to suggest that a professional has made a mistake (misdiagnosed) is not libel since anyone can make one mistake and professionals are not expected to be perfect.

Sixth Amendment – In all criminal prosecutions, the accused shall enjoy the right to a speedy and public trial, by an impartial jury of the State and district wherein the crime shall have been committed, which district shall have been previously ascertained by law, and to be informed of the nature and cause of the accusation; to be confronted with the witnesses against him; to have compulsory process for obtaining witnesses in his favor, and to have the Assistance of Counsel for his defence.

SLAPP Suit – a recent phenomenon in which targets of media criticism file SLAPP [strategic law suits against public participation] to discourage journalistic publication; not intended to win, just to create expense and serve as a warning that publishing controversial material could result in an expensive suit. Some states have anti-SLAPP laws to discourage the practice.

Social Responsibility theory of the press –
developed largely in the 20th century due to growing
criticism of the media and the inability of libertarian to
function effectively. Basis of theory grew out of the
writings of the Commission on Freedom of the Press,
funded by Time's Henry Luce following
WWII. Known as the Hutchins
Commission. Produced two important works in 1947:
Commission Report, A Free & Responsible Press; and
William Hocking's Freedom of Press: A Framework of
Principle.

Sonny Bono Act – see Copyright Term Extension Act

Sources of American Law – Common law, Statutory
law, Constitutional law, Administrative law, and
Executive law

Soviet Communist theory of the press – under the
old soviet system, media were owned by the state and
existed as an arm of government to advance the goals
or interests of the state.

Special Damages – in a libel award damages for
specific monetary loss; a more precise damage than in
actual and requires a higher level of verification.

State Open Meetings and Open Records Laws – all
50 states now have both open meetings and open
records acts providing umbrella protections to
maintain openness in local and state
governments. Generally, all meetings are open except
parole boards, mental health agencies, adoption
agencies, law enforcement agencies, hospital boards,
etc.

Most states require meeting notices, allow executive
sessions and have exemptions including such things as
personnel matters, real estate transactions, legal cases
involving the agency, and matters involving public
safety. In most states, all records of specific agencies
including schools, cities etc. (not courts) are open.
Common exemptions include:

1. Information classified by state or federal law
2. Law enforcement information
3. Trade secrets
4. Preliminary departmental memos/drafts
5. Personal information
6. Litigation

Stare Decisis – let the decision stand. Common law
or law based on precedent.

Statute of Limitations – time limit for filing suit,
usually 1-3 years. In North Carolina, a libel suit, for
example, must be filed within one year. (May sue in
any state in which the libel is published/broadcast. So,
if the statute of limitations has expired in one state, it
is possible to file in a state with longer period).

Statutory Construction - Court's role in statutory law
is called statutory construction or the interpretation of
a particular law and its legislative intent.

Statutory Law – Legislative law, laws passed by
Congress, state legislatures, city councils etc.

Strict Liability – concept in law in which a defendant
would be held responsible for damages to an
individual without proof of fault; existed in libel law

prior to *Times v. Sullivan, Curtis v. Butts,* and *Gertz v. Welch.*

Summary Judgment – procedure by which a lawsuit is ended prior to a trial. In a libel case, for example, if a plaintiff cannot make a clear case for one of the requirements (publication, identification, defamation, falsity or fault), the judge may issue a summary judgment for the defendant. Three-fourths or more of all libel cases end in summary judgment. Request is filed after plaintiff has filed written arguments and before the trial begins.

The defendant must show either:

1. Plaintiff failed to make a case for either publication, identification, defamation, falsity, or fault.
2. There is a legal defense (statute of limitations, privilege, fair comment etc.)

TTTTT

Telecommunications Act of 1996 - major revision of the 1934 Communications Act, which among other things has the following results:

1. Removes all limits on the number of television and radio stations that can be owned by a single entity as long as the television stations do no reach an audience of more than 39 % (per revision/originally 35 %) of the U.S. television households

2. Removes limits, which prevented one entity from owning both a radio station and a television station in the same market -- in the top 50 markets

3.Extended renewal period to 8 years for both radio and television stations

4. Eliminated the regulation of rates for most cable services.
5. Attempted to impose the Communications Decency Act to limit "indecent" materials on the internet. . . ruled unconstitutional in *Reno v. ACLU*.

6. Requires microchips, which allow parents to block unwanted content.

Teleological – consequence based view; holds all things to be designed for or directed toward a final result, that there is an inherent purpose or final cause for all that exists. Utilitarianism is a teleological way of looking at things: the best actions is that which does the greatest good for the greatest number.

Theories of/about First Amendment – following are some of the most common theories of First Amendment intent:

1. Absolutist Theory – absolute or literal interpretation of the "no law" statement. Nothing should infringe on 1st Amendment rights. If other rights conflict, 1st takes priority. Impractical in that some things fall outside of 1st Am protection, i.e., child porn, defamation, obscenity, threats etc.

2. Ad hoc balancing Theory (Strategy) – (ad hoc = case at hand) balancing 1st Amendment freedoms against other rights on a case by case basis (i.e., free press v. fair trial etc.)

3. Preferred Position Balancing Theory – in balancing free expression with other rights, it is assumed that any limitation on speech or press is illegal. Free speech will be preferred; and other party must justify an infringement. Based on belief that the maintenance of all rights is based on freedom of speech and press.

4. Meiklejohnian Theory – 1. Speech related to the self-governing process receives absolute protection [maximum scrutiny] 2. Speech not related to self-governing process balanced w/other rights. [minimum/intermediate scrutiny]

Time, Place, Manner Restrictions (TPM) – narrowly defined free speech/expression restrictions based on factors other than content (content neutral). Must pass intermediate scrutiny consideration.

Total Public figure – for purposes of libel law, a total public figure is someone who is instantly recognizable; of such a celebrity status that pretty much anyone would know who they are; required to prove actual malice in a libel suit.

Tort – civil wrongdoing giving injured party legal remedy in civil court: invasion of privacy, libel, trespass, negligence etc.

Trade Libel – intentional disparagement of the quality of a product, resulting in monetary loss.

Trademark – word, symbol, device or combination of the three that differentiates a company's goods and services from those of competitors. May include such things as:

1. Trade names – Pepsi, Macintosh, Crayola, etc.
2. Shapes – Coca-Cola bottle, Chrysler building spire in NYC
3. Slogans – "All the News That's Fit to Print," "Uh-huh" (Pepsi)
4. Telephone Number – 1-800-FLOWERS
5. Color – pink of a particular fiberglass insulation
6. Trade dress –color/design – Pepsi can, dictionary etc.

Transformative - in copyright law, a work that is based on an original copyrighted work but with an added new element for the purpose of a parody; protected under fair use

Trial Courts – civil or criminal court where most cases begin; hears evidence and determines facts of the case.

True Threat – defined as words that target an individual or small group, are intended to convey a real threat of impending physical harm, and are intended to arouse pervasive fear of violence in targeted individuals

Twibel – libel by twitter; originally associated with a libel lawsuit against Coutney Love for disparaging comment made online.

UUUUU

United States Supreme Court – the highest court in the U.S. court system; established in 1789; comprised of one Chief Justice of the United States and eight associate justices, all appointed by the President of the United States, with Senate approval. Current members of the Court are Chief Justice John Roberts and Associate Justices Samuel Alito, Clarence Thomas, Anthony Kennedy, Stephen Breyer, Ruth Bader Ginsburg, Elena Kagan, Sonia Sotomayor, and Neil Gorsuch.

USA Patriot Act, 2001 – (Uniting & Strengthening America by Providing Appropriate Tools Required to Intercept & Obstruct Terrorism Act of 2001)

1. expanded authority of FBI to issue National Security Letters requiring businesses to turn over customer records (and not tell customer)
2. sharing of grand jury information
3. sharing of contents of wire, oral and electronic communications obtained by law enforcement
4. access to stored voice mail
5. expanded power to access electronic communications
6. greater authority to trace internet communications
7. greater power regarding search warrants

8. Reapproved in 2006 with rewrites/civil liberty safeguards

USSC – United States Supreme Court

Utilitarianism - the best action is that which produces the greatest amount of good (or pleasure) for the largest number of people . . . requires computing the consequences of action for all involved.

> **Act utilitarianism** - situational - deals with a specific case, does a particular act result in a balance of good over evil

> **Rule utilitarianism** - looks at generalities attempting to construct moral rules that promote the greatest general welfare

VVVVV

V-Chip – device required to be installed on all television sets 13 inches and larger manufactured after Jan. 1, 2000 to allow families to program the TV to block out specific content based on a ratings system . . . including violence, sex, and language.

Voir Dire – the questioning of jurors in the pre-trial process; a compensatory remedy for prejudicial publicity in which potential jurors with bias or prejudice are excused from serving on the jury. (for cause, peremptory)

WWWWW

Wireless Ship Act, 1910 – Congress ruled that all U.S. passenger ships had to carry a radio.

Wire service defense – libel defense; not responsible if received from a reputable news-gathering agency, did not know story was false, nothing in story to make suspect, and no substantial changes to the original.

Works for Hire – when working for someone else and you create a copyrightable work, unless there is an agreement to the contrary the work belongs to the employer; works for hire are protected for either 95 years from publication or 120 years from creation.

World Intellectual Property Organization – an agency of the United Nations; conference in 1996 adopted treaties granting copyright owners protection for distribution of their works in digital form (includes art, literature, film, computer software, and recorded music). WIPO administers the Berne Convention and the Universal Copyright Convention

ZZZZZ

Zapple Rule – appearance by supporters of one candidate does not trigger equal time to other candidates, but does require equal time to supporters of other candidates.

Zone of privacy – those areas assumed to be protected from search or intrusion without a proper search warrant; your home, property, papers etc.; continually challenged by public officials, law enforcement and the courts; recent USSC decisions, for example, declare that police may not attach a gps to a private vehicle (U.S. v. Jones) or examine a private cell phone (Riley v. California) without a search warrant.

Studying for Exams

The following pages contain an index of material covered in the Media Law & Ethics course taught by the author. Separated into those things covered by Exams 1, 2, and 3, it is further organized into three distinct areas: 1. cases, 2. terms and phrases, and 3. concepts and listings. Every item listed in these pages is detailed in either the Case Summaries or Terms, Concepts, and Theories sections.

Please note that those two sections contain more information than is listed here and that students may not be required to know all that is contained therein for exams.

Please also note that while every effort has been made to make this index as complete as possible, there occasionally may be materials added during a given semester, which do not appear here.

Exam # 1

Introduction to Media Law

Cases:

Gitlow v. New York, 1925
Marbury v. Madison, 1803
Cohen v. California, 1971
U.S. v. O'Brien, 1968
Texas v. Johnson, 1989
Near v. Minnesota, 1931

N.Y. Times v. U.S., 1971 (Pentagon Papers)
Tinker v. Des Moines, 1969
Bethel School District v. Fraser, 1986
Hazelwood v. Kuhlmeier, 1988
Morse v. Frederick, 2007
Doninger v. Niehoff, 2009
Layshock v. Hermitage School District, 2011
Evans v. Bayer, 2010
J.S. v. Blue Mountain School District, 2011
Kowalski v. Berkely County Schools, 2011
Bell v. Itawamba, 2016
Wynar v. Douglas, 2013
Lovell v. Griffin, 1938
U.S. v. Eichman / U.S. v. Haggerty, 1990
Chaplinsky v. New Hampshire, 1942
Gooding v. Wilson, 1972
Village of Skokie v. National Socialist Party, 1978
Terminiello v. Chicago, 1949
R.A.V. v. St. Paul, 1992
Virginia v. Black, 2003
Elonis v. U.S., 2015
Schenck v. U.S., 1919
Brandenburg v. Ohio, 1969
McCullen v. Coakley, 2014
Packingham v. North Carolina, 2017
Virginia State Bd. of Education v. Barnette, 1943

Terms/phrases:

1st Amendment
4th Amendment
6th Amendment
9th Amendment

14th Amendment
Law (definition)
Custom of the Court
Precedent
Stare decisis
Doctrine of precedent
Statutory construction / legislative intent
Civil law / criminal law
Jurisdiction
Trial Courts
Appellate Courts
Original jurisdiction
Appellate jurisdiction
Direct Appeal
Writ of certiorari
Plaintiff / Defendant
Per curiam decision
Memorandum order/opinion
Judicial review
Originalist / non-originalist
Textualist / Intentionalist
Jefferson's Wall of separation
Judicial restraint/judicial activism
Characteristics of USSC
Prior restraint
Presumption of constitutionality
Preferred position doctrine
Time, Place, Manner Restrictions (content based
v. content neutral)
John Milton
Areopagitica

Concepts/listings:

Difference between law and ethics
Differences between common and statutory laws

Sources of Law:
1. Common Law
2. Statutory Law
3. Constitutional Law
4. Administrative Law
5. Executive Law

State Courts:
Trial courts of limited jurisdiction (traffic)
Trial courts of general jurisdiction (county)
Court of Appeals - intermediary
State Supreme Court

Federal Courts:
U.S. District Courts (94, every state has at least one)
U.S. Court of Appeals (13 circuits)
U.S. Supreme Court

United States Supreme Court: (established 1789)
Composed of nine members: one Chief Justice of the U.S. and eight associate justices. Appointed by the president with Senate approval . . . for life.

How does SC decide which cases to hear? Looks for broad questions of national importance, i.e., abortion, civil rights, criminal rights etc.; cases where lower courts disagree

U.S. Supreme Court Justices:

Chief Justice John Roberts
Brett Kavanaugh
Clarence Thomas
Ruth Bader Ginsburg
Stephen Breyer
Samuel Alito
Sonia Sotamayor
Elena Kagan
Neil Gorsuch.

Theories of First Amendment Intent / How it is or might be applied

1. Absolutist Theory
2. Ad hoc balancing Theory
3. Preferred Position Balancing Theory
4. Meiklejohnian Theory

Functions of / Reasons for First Amendment

1. Discovery of Truth in the Marketplace / Libertarianism
2. Access Leading to Participation in Democracy
3. Watchdog/Check on Government
4. Self-realization/self-fulfillment
5. Safety valve/social stability theory

Application of the First Amendment (Miscellaneous)

1. Protected from state infringement by interpretation of 14th Amendment in *Gitlow v. New York*, 1925. (Extends to local governments as well.)

2. First Amendment applies to governmental interference. "Private" schools, businesses are not similarly prevented from interfering with speech/press.

3. First Amendment protects all forms of speech: verbal, symbolic, and expressive conduct (that which communicates an idea . . . expressive conduct that is otherwise illegal is not protected . . . i.e. throwing rocks at the windows of an army recruitment office to protest military policies.)

4. Entertainment intended to communicate an idea is protected: movies to nude dancing.

5. First Amendment also protects the right to NOT: speak, practice religion etc.

6. While the right to disseminate information is largely absolute, there can be limits on the right to gather information.

Levels of Scrutiny (Limitations on the First Amendment):

Minimum Scrutiny (Rational basis) - Unprotected speech (low value, not worthy of protections, i.e. obscenity, libel, fighting words, false advertising, etc.)

Intermediate Scrutiny - Protected speech with limits (truthful commercial advertising, content neutral restrictions on time, place and manner)

Restrictions on expressive conduct when directed at the conduct

Strict Scrutiny - Protected Speech (political speech, personal expression) Content based TPM restrictions

Types of Public Forum:

Traditional
Limited/designated
Public property not public forum
Private property as public forum

Censorship in schools (public v. private / high school v. university)

1. A school sponsored newspaper produced as a part of a class most likely to be subject to censorship.
2. A paper produced in the school as an extracurricular activity also may be subject to censorship.
3. A paper produced and distributed off campus not subject to censorship. Can be banned from campus, but students cannot be punished. .
. likewise, school cannot punish a student for comments made about the school on a personal web site.

\Criteria for Censoring High School Newspaper That
Is Part of a Class:

> 1.Material which interferes with school
> discipline—disruption.
> 2.Material which interferes with rights of students
> – privacy, defamation etc. Material not meeting
> standards of academic propriety – grammar etc.
> 3.Material causing health/welfare concerns:
> tobacco, alcohol. Obscene or vulgar materials.

Off-campus / online speech
Censorship in secondary private schools
Censorship of College Newspapers / public v. private
Flag Burning
Flag Protection Act, 1989
Constitutional Amendment Process
Fighting Words
Hate speech and true threat
What Constitutes a True Threat?
Clear & Present Danger / Incitement to Violence
Brandenburg Test

Libel Law

Cases:

> Hepps v. Philadelphia Inquirer, 1986 (media v.
> non-media)
> New York Times v. Sullivan, 1964
> Curtis v. Butts/AP v. Walker, 1967
> Gertz v. Welch, 1974
> Time v. Firestone, 1976
> Milkovich v. Lorain Journal, 1991

Cubby v. Compuserv, 1991
Stratton Oakmont v. Prodigy, 1995
Zeran v. America Online, 1998
Doe v. Cahill, 2005

Terms/phrases/concepts:

Libel
Tort/Civil complaint
Slander
Plaintiff
Defendant
Defamation
Re-publication
Group Identification
Strict liability
Libel per se
Libel per quod
Actual malice
Public official
Simple negligence
All purpose or total public figure
Limited public figure
Summary Judgment
Test for reckless disregard for the truth
Libel in Cyberspace (cyber-libel, Twibel)
Good Samaritan provision of the Telecom
Act/Section 230

Listings

Plaintiff's Case:

1. Publication

2. Identification
3. Defamation/harm
4. Falsity
5.Fault

Defendant's Case (defenses):

1. Conditional or qualified privilege
2. Rhetorical Hyperbole
3. Fair Comment

Secondary Defenses:

1. Statute of Limitations
2. Right-of-reply
3. Retraction
4. Wire service defense
5. Libel-proof plaintiff
6. Neutral reporting

Types of damages:

1. Actual Damages
2. Special Damages
3. Presumed Damages
4. Punitive Damages

Other Important Points:

1. Any living person may bring a libel suit
2. Survivors of a deceased plaintiff may continue a libel suit, begun before the individual's death
3. Business or non-profits may sue if they can show loss of public support
4. Governmental bodies may not sue for libel.

Exam # 2

Invasion of Privacy

Cases:

Roberson v. Rochester Folding Box Co., 1902
Pavesich v. New England Mutual Life, 1905
Midler v. Ford, 1988
Cox v. Cohn, 1975
Dieteman v. Time Inc., 1971
Leverton v. Curtis Pub. Co., 1951
Time v. Hill, 1967
Hustler v. Falwell, 1988
Riley v. California, 2014
Carpenter v. U.S., 2018
Maryland v. King, 2013
Florida v. Jardines, 2013
Florida v. Harris, 2013
U.S. v. Jones, 2012
Griswold v. Connecticut, 1965
Lawrence v. Texas, 2003
Byrd v. United States, 2018
Collins v. Virginia, 2018

Terms/phrases/concepts:

Privacy
Right of privacy
Right of publicity
Incidental Use
Booth Rule

Consent as a defense
Intentional infliction of emotional distress
Publicity/publication in privacy law
Reasonable expectation of privacy
Zone of privacy
Constitutional roots of privacy
Electronic Communication Privacy Act
Children's Online Privacy Protection Act
USA Patriot Act
Privacy Act of 1974

Listings:

Categories of invasion of privacy:

1. Appropriation
2. Publication of private information
3. Intrusion
4. False light

Government transparency:

Daniel Ellsberg,
Julian Assange,
Chelsea Manning,
Edward Snowden

Access to Places & Information

Cases:

Zemel v. Rusk, 1964
Pell v. Procunier / Saxbe v. Wash. Post, 1974

Houchins v. KQED, 1975
Wilson v. Layne / Hanlon v. Berger, 1999
U.S. v. Jones, 2012
Riley v. California, 2014
Carpenter v. U.S., 2018

Terms/phrases/concepts:

Right to gather information vs. right to disseminate
Reporters and private property
Reporters and ride-alongs
Freedom of Information Act
Electronic FOIA
Federal Sunshine Act
State Open Meetings Laws
State Open Records Laws

Media & the Justice System

Cases:

Estes v. Texas, 1965
Chandler v. Florida, 1981
KQED v. Vasquez, 1991
Sheppard v. Maxwell, 1966
Gannett v. DesPasquale, 1979
Richmond Newspapers v. Virginia, 1980
Press Enterprise v. Riverside Superior Court (I and II), 1984/1986
Branzburg v. Hayes (also in re Pappas & U.S. v. Caldwell), 1972
Risen v. U.S., 2013

Terms/phrases/concepts:

Prejudicial publicity
Contempt power
Summary contempt power
Civil contempt
Direct criminal contempt
Indirect criminal contempt
The Conflict: First Amendment v. Sixth
Amendment
ABA Canon 35
Hauptman trial
Free Flow of Information Act
Shield laws
Dickinson Rule
Reardon Report

Listings:

Types of things the ABA considers prejudicial

1. Confessions
2. Lie detector results
3. Stories on defendant's past criminal record
4. Stories questioning credibility of witnesses
5. Stories about a defendant's character
6. Stories that tend to inflame the public mood against a defendant
7. Stories that suggest or declare that a defendant is guilty

Compensatory remedies for prejudicial publicity

1. Voir Dire
2. Change of venue / change of verniremen
3. Continuance
4. Admonition
5. Sequestration

Controlling remedies

1. Restrictive (Gag) order
2. Trial closures

Copyright/Creative Property

Cases:

Eldred v. Ashcroft, 2003
Feist Publications v. Rural Telephone Service Co.,
Inc., 1991
Miller v. Universal Studios, 1981
Harper & Row v. Nation, 1985
Campbell v. Acuff-Rose Music, 1984
A&M Records v. Napster, 2001
MGM v. Grokster, 2005
Rogers v. Koons, 1992
Basic Books v. Kinkos, 1991

Terms/phrases/concepts:

Copyright – body of law dealing with intangible
property (intellectual property), which exists to
protect the original/intellectual creations of

authors, composers, artists, inventors, playwrights etc.

Patents
Trademarks
Lanham Act
Constitutional basis of copyright law
Duration of ownership
1976 law (took effect Jan. 1, 1978)
Bono Act (CTEA-Copyright Term Extension Act)
Materials which cannot by copyrighted
Compilation
Collective Works
Derivative Works
Transformative work
Parody
Work for hire
Unfair competition/misappropriation
Fair use doctrine
Copyright notice
The World Intellectual Property Organization
Berne convention
Digital Millennium Copyright Act
Creative Commons

Listings:

What kinds of work are protected by copyright law under the 1976 law?

1. literary works
2. musical works, including any accompanying words

3. dramatic works, including any accompanying music
4. pantomimes and choreographic works
5. pictorial, graphic, and sculptural works
6. motion pictures and other audiovisual works
7. sound recordings
8. architectural works

Exclusive rights in copyrighted works

1. Right to reproduce
2. Right to make derivative works
3. Right to distribute the work publicly
4. Right to publicly perform
5. Right to publicly display
6.Right to transmit

Criteria for determining fair use

1. Purpose and character of use
2. Nature of copyrighted material
3. Amount and substantiality of use
4. Economic impact of use

Broadcast Licensing & Content

Cases:

Red Lion Broadcasting v. FCC, 1969
Miami Herald v. Tornillo, 1974
UCC v. FCC, 1966
CBS v. FCC, 1981
FCC v. Pacifica, 1978
Fox v. FCC, 2009, 2012

Terms/phrases/concepts:

Network v. local v. cable
Deregulation
Ascertainment
Why regulate broadcasting?
PICON
Wireless Ship Act, 1910
Radio Act of 1912
Radio Act of 1927
Communications Act of 1934
Telecommunications Act of 1996
Powers of the FCC
License Renewal process
Multiple Ownership Rules (nationally & within a single market)
Candidate Access Rule
Equal Time/Equal Opportunity Rule
Equal Time exemptions
Fairness Doctrine
Personal Attack Rule
Political Editorials Rule
Children's Television Act 1990
Rules limiting ads per minute
Safe harbor policy
Broadcast Decency Enforcement Act
V-chip
Net neutrality

Exam # 3

Obscenity/Indecency

Cases:

Butler v. Michigan, 1957
Roth v. U.S., 1957
Memoirs v. Mass., 1966
Miller v. California, 1973
Hamling v. U.S., 1974
Pinkus v. U.S., 1978
Pope v. Illinois, 1987
New York v. Ferber, 1982
U.S. v. Williams, 2008
Reno v. ACLU, 1997
Ashcroft v. ACLU/Gonzales v. ACLU, 2007
U.S. v. American Library Association, 2003
Ashcroft v. Free Speech Coalition, 2002
Matal v. Tam, 2018

Terms/phrases/concepts:

Obscenity
Indecent Material
Indecency
Pornography
Local, state and federal laws
Postal regulations
Customs regulations
Comstock Law (1873)
Hicklin Rule
Child Pornography Prevention Act of 1996

PROTECT Act
Communication Decency Act
Child Online Protection Act
Children's Internet Protection Act

Advertising/Commercial Speech

Cases:

Valentine v. Chrestensen, 1942
Times v. Sullivan, 1964
Pittsburgh Press v. Pitts. Commission on Human
Relations, 1973
Bigelow v. Virginia, 1975
Virginia State Board of Pharmacy v. Va. Citizens
Consumer Council, 1976
Central Hudson Gas & Electric v. Public Service
Commission of NY, 1980

Terms/phrases/concepts:

Commercial Speech Doctrine
Central Hudson test
Means of regulating advertising industry
Federal Trade commission
Advertising defined
Requirement for the FTC to become involved in
regulation of advertising
FTC remedies (guides, voluntary orders, consent
agreements, substantiation, corrective ads,
injunctions, trade rules)
Lanham Act
Expert Endorsements

Influencer Marketing
FTC Endorsement Guidelines
Publisher Liability

Listings:

In order for advertising to be considered false or deceptive:

1. There must be a representation, omission, or practice that is likely to mislead the consumer.
2. The act or practice must be considered from the perspective of a consumer who is acting reasonably.
3. The representation, omission, or practice must be material. (It's ok, for example, to use perfectly formed plastic ice cubes in an adv. for soft drinks, but not in an adv. for ice cubes.

Media Ethics

Ethical Conduct - Conduct or behavior which is right or which conforms to the standards of a given society at a given time . . . conduct which is good out of a sense of moral conviction rather than from a fear of punishment.

Metaethics, Normative & Applied ethics, Egalitarianism

Stages of the Potter Box Decision-Making Formula

1. Situation, 2. Values, 3. Principles, 4. Loyalties, 5. Decision

<u>Applying Principles to Ethical Decision-Making:</u>

1. Aristotle's Golden Mean - Theory that the moral virtue is a mean between two extremes.

2. Kant's Categorical Imperative - "Act on that maxim which you will to become a universal law." . . . . or make a decision in a manner you wish similar situations to be decided. (deontological - rule or duty based)

3. Mill's Principle of Utility - seeking the greatest happiness for the greatest number. Utilitarianism - the best action is that which produces the greatest amount of good for the largest number of people . . . requires computing the consequences of action for all involved. (teleological - consequence based)

4. Rawl's Veil of Ignorance - justice emerges when negotiating without social distinctions.

5. Judeo-Christian Concept of Agape - unselfish love, "love your neighbor as yourself," accepting a person's existence as it is; to love him or her as is . . .blind, non-discriminating love.

<u>Four Theories of the Press</u>

1. Authoritarian - Under the authoritarian system, the press is controlled (not owned) in function and operation by an organized society through the institution of government. It is controlled in order to prevent it from interfering with the goals of the state.

2. Soviet Communist - under the old soviet system, media were owned by the state and existed as an arm of government to advance the goals or interests of the state.

3. Libertarian - developed in 17th - 18th century England. It was believed that: Man is a rational being and is capable of making decisions to advance his own interests. Society or state exists to allow the individual to accomplish his objectives. Relative to intellectual pursuit, man is rational and thus capable of discovering truth on his own.

The press system in a libertarian society would be uncontrolled/unregulated.

The open marketplace of ideas . . . in which everyone is allowed to speak as it is believed that the truth will rise to the top . . . the self-righting process ... even if falsity gains temporary victory, truth will eventually win out. (Milton's Areopagitica)

4. Social Responsibility - developed largely in the 20th century due to growing criticism of the media and the inability of libertarian to function effectively.

Basis of the social responsibility theory grew out of the writings of the Commission on Freedom of the Press, funded by Time's Henry Luce following WWII. Known as the Hutchins Commission.

Produced two important works in 1947: *Commission Report, A Free & Responsible Press*; and William Hocking's *Freedom of Press: A Framework of Principle.*

Nature of man (the individual) in social responsibility theory vs. libertarianism:

1. libertarian - rational
2. social responsibility - not irrational, but lazy (or extremely busy) and therefore needing media help in interpreting news

Five Things Which Society Requires of its Press

1. To provide a truthful, comprehensive and intelligent account of the day's events in a context that gives them meaning.
2. Forum for exchange of comment and criticism.
3. Representative picture of constituent groups.
4. Be responsible for the presentation and clarification of the goals of society.
5. Provide full access to the day's intelligence.

Other terms, phrase, misc.:

Elements of Journalism
Committee of Concerned Journalists
Society of Professional Journalists
Public Relations Society of America
American Society of Newspaper Editors

Hypotheticals

Responding to hypotheticals is one of the more reliable tests of what you have learned in this course. It is where you get to apply what you have learned to practical/realistic situations involving legal and/or ethical issues. In most cases, you are asked to read about a situation and respond by indicating what a judge or court would likely do based on a precedent case. And yes, you will be asked to cite that court case. That's why you memorized all those cases. Some of the cases appearing on the following pages will be graded assignments, others just for in-class discussion. Other, similar hypotheticals will appear on each of the three major exams.

Hypothetical # 1

The f*** Word Can Get You in Some Deep S***(Or Can It??)

You and your friends are out enjoying a Saturday night in downtown Elon. The hour is late when an Elon police officer approaches you to suggest, "It's time to get off the streets and go on home."

You reply that you're not ready to go home. After a few more exchanges, things heat up and you say: "Fuck you cop. I'm not fucking going home. It's none of your fucking business when I go home." The nice policeman proceeds to arrest you for disturbing the peace, offensive language, and maybe even fighting words.

What are your chances in court? Cite precedents. You may cite as many lower court decisions as you like, but please cite at least one relevant USSC decision. One page maximum typed with sources.

Hypothetical # 2

Careful What You Tweet, It Might Come Back to Bite You

You're getting in some serious study time in the Oak Room for a Media Law exam when you overhear a conversation about one of your professors and a student in your class.

"They were all over each other last night at the Lion's Den (a bar downtown)," one person said.

"I heard Professor Bell was high when she came in. She went right over to Patrick Jones, bought two beers and started coming on to him. They left together about an hour later," the second person said. "And she was seen coming out of the Oaks this morning."

Later that night, you tweet, "Popular history prof whose name rhymes with jell, gets high and hooks up with underage male cutie." Turns out Professor Bell was at a conference in NYC. When she hears about the tweet, she's very upset and meets with an attorney.

Does she have a case? Discuss, considering the 5 requirements for proving libel and any precedent cases.

Hypothetical # 3

Red Wine, Lady Chaplain & An Embarrassing Sidewalk Sprawl

You operate a popular Twitter account called Elon Juice in which you tweet about campus gossip, rumors, and the juiciest tales about administration and faculty you can imagine. Your trusty iPhone is always on call.

On this day, you are chillin' at the new Oak Room when you see the University chaplain and the director of Hillel at a table near you. There's a half full glass of red wine setting in front of the chaplain. Just as she picks it up to take a sip you shoot a photo.

Fifteen or so minutes later you've moved to a bench outside looking for better "juice." Just as you're about to call it a day, you see the chaplain coming through the door. She stumbles at the Oak Room exit and sprawls awkwardly on the sidewalk. Just as she looks up from her unfortunate position on the ground you shoot a second photo. Later you tweet both photos (the one of the Chaplain sipping wine and the other one with her sprawling on the sidewalk). The accompanying tweet says simply, "Lady Chaplain Has One Too Many."

Consider both libel and privacy issues. Are you invading her privacy in any way? Discuss. List and explain any precedent cases.

Hypothetical # 4

Art Is in the Eye of the Beholder, But Is It Breaking the Law?

You are a student in a college art class. You are assigned to create a project that expresses a political point of view. Without telling your instructor what you plan to do, you go to Target and purchase an American flag. Back in the studio, you cut the flag into 15 or so squares, rearrange the pieces and rough stitch it all back together.

Then using a screen printer, you superimpose a photo of a city slum scene over the fabric, with the following title: "Decaying America." You post it with the other student projects, but when the instructor comes in later she tells you that you must take it down, that you are breaking a state law preventing flag desecration, and that you and she could get in big trouble.

How do you respond? Is she right? Cite a case that applies.

Hypothetical # 5

To Talk or Not to Talk, That Is the Question

As an intern for the local daily newspaper, you have been working on an investigative story on cocaine use by athletes at your university. One of your key sources, a well-known basketball player has identified some 35 users as well as their on-campus supplier.

Not long after the article is published, a raid and subsequent arrest results in a trial in which you are called to testify. The court wants to know where you got your information. Unfortunately, your source for the story provided you with information only after you promised him that you would not reveal his identity.

What do you do? What happens if you refuse to provide the information requested? List any precedent case.

Hypothetical # 6

Hard Work Always Pays Off, Or Does It?

For the past three months, you have been investigating a group of older students and townspeople you believe are selling drugs and running an illegal gambling game on campus. You take a rough draft of an article to an editor at the campus newspaper. You are told it looks good but that you need to get at least a couple more sources to verify some of the information.

You continue working on the article, but on the following evening a Greensboro TV station airs a similar story containing the same information as is in your article. You know that one of the editors at the campus newspaper is interning at the station, in fact the same editor that said your article looks good. You suspect she repackaged your facts and gave it to the station.

What recourse do you have? Can you sue for copyright infringement? Why? Why not? Cite any relevant cases you can find.

Hypothetical # 7

When A Doll in a Pinstriped Suit & A Serious Case of "Dumb" Overcome Rational Behavior

You pick up a couple hotdogs, your favorite drink, and a copy of the "Slammer" at the local Kangaroo Express and head back to your room. While thumbing through this tabloid of local arrests you spot a photo of a middle-aged refined-looking woman who looks somewhat out-of-place in this sea of three-day old beards, scraggly hair, and Justin Bieber lookalikes.

You look down at the name and address: Lucille Floogle, 2222 Pembroke Drive, arrested for shoplifting. You recognize the address as that of University President Lester Floogle. Excitement builds. You may just have that scoop you need to get an A in your news reporting class. You pick up your phone, dial the university operator and ask for the number of President Floogle's residence. The operator hesitates, but does give you the number when you tell her you're working on an article for class and possibly the campus newspaper.

You dial the number and the president's wife picks up on the third ring. "Hello, this is Lucille," she says. You explain who you are and why you are calling. "I'm calling about the shoplifting arrest," you say. She immediately launches into the following explanation laced with numerous requests that you not write about it. "I was shopping for a birthday present for my grandson. He's turning three and loves the High Achiever boy dolls at Target. Lester had seen the latest doll, "The Wall Street Wonder," cutest little boy doll with his pinstriped suit and tiny brief case. I just had to have it. When I got to Target there was only one left on the shelf, so I grabbed it and headed to checkout. About the time I reached the front of the store, I realized I had no cash and had left all my credit cards at home.

I was afraid if I put it back someone else would buy it before I returned. So, I made a bad decision. I stuffed the doll down into my oversized purse and proceeded to walk out the door. I would rush home, pick up my wallet, return to the store and once inside take the doll out of my purse and go through checkout. Good intentions. No harm done." Of course, the alarm rang on Mrs. Floogle, a security officer found the doll in her purse, called the police and she was arrested for shoplifting. She asks again that you not write about her arrest; not print it in the campus newspaper. You're still convinced you have a great GPA building story and don't want to give it up.

What do you do? Use the Potter Box to analyze the situation and make a decision.

Professional Ethics Codes

Following is a collection of ethical codes from select professional media organizations such as the Society of Professional Journalists, the American Society of Newspaper Editors, the Radio Television Digital News Association, the Public Relations Society of America, and the National Photographers Association.

Additionally, a copy of the NPR Handbook is included as a sample of media ethics codes. Most major news organizations such as Associate Press, The New York Times, The Washington Post etc. also have codes available online by Googling the organization.

Society of Professional Journalists Code of Ethics

Preamble

Members of the Society of Professional Journalists believe that public enlightenment is the forerunner of justice and the foundation of democracy. The duty of the journalist is to further those ends by seeking truth and providing a fair and comprehensive account of events and issues. Conscientious journalists from all media and specialties strive to serve the public with thoroughness and honesty. Professional integrity is the cornerstone of a journalist's credibility. Members of the Society share a dedication to ethical behavior and adopt this code to declare the Society's principles and standards of practice.

Seek Truth and Report It

Journalists should be honest, fair and courageous in gathering, reporting and interpreting information. Journalists should:

1. Test the accuracy of information from all sources and exercise care to avoid inadvertent error. Deliberate distortion is never permissible.
2. Diligently seek out subjects of news stories to give them the opportunity to respond to allegations of wrongdoing.

3. Identify sources whenever feasible. The public is entitled to as much information as possible on sources' reliability.

4. Always question sources' motives before promising anonymity. Clarify conditions attached to any promise made in exchange for information. Keep promises.

5. Make certain that headlines, news teases and promotional material, photos, video, audio, graphics, sound bites and quotations do not misrepresent. They should not oversimplify or highlight incidents out of context.

6. Never distort the content of news photos or video. Image enhancement for technical clarity is always permissible. Label montages and photo illustrations.

7. Avoid misleading re-enactments or staged news events. If re-enactment is necessary to tell a story, label it.

8. Avoid undercover or other surreptitious methods of gathering information except when traditional open methods will not yield information vital to the public. Use of such methods should be explained as part of the story

9. Never plagiarize.

10. Tell the story of the diversity and magnitude of the human experience boldly, even when it is unpopular to do so.

11. Examine their own cultural values and avoid imposing those values on others.

12. Avoid stereotyping by race, gender, age, religion, ethnicity, geography, sexual orientation, disability, physical appearance or social status.

13. Support the open exchange of views, even views they find repugnant.

14. Give voice to the voiceless; official and unofficial sources of information can be equally valid.

15. Distinguish between advocacy and news reporting. Analysis and commentary should be labeled and not misrepresent fact or context.

16. Distinguish news from advertising and shun hybrids that blur the lines between the two.

17. Recognize a special obligation to ensure that the public's business is conducted in the open and that government records are open to inspection.

Minimize Harm

Ethical journalists treat sources, subjects and colleagues as human beings deserving of respect. Journalists should:

1. Show compassion for those who may be affected adversely by news coverage. Use special sensitivity when dealing with children and inexperienced sources or subjects.

2. Be sensitive when seeking or using interviews or photographs of those affected by tragedy or grief.

3. Recognize that gathering and reporting information may cause harm or discomfort. Pursuit of the news is not a license for arrogance.

4. Recognize that private people have a greater right to control information about themselves than do public officials and others who seek power,

influence or attention. Only an overriding public need can justify intrusion into anyone's privacy.
5. Show good taste. Avoid pandering to lurid curiosity.
6. Be cautious about identifying juvenile suspects or victims of sex crimes.
7. Be judicious about naming criminal suspects before the formal filing of charges.
8. Balance a criminal suspect's fair trial rights with the public's right to be informed.

Act Independently

Journalists should be free of obligation to any interest other than the public's right to know. Journalists should:

1. Avoid conflicts of interest, real or perceived.
2. Remain free of associations and activities that may compromise integrity or damage credibility.
3. Refuse gifts, favors, fees, free travel and special treatment, and shun secondary employment, political involvement, public office and service in community organizations if they compromise journalistic integrity.
4. Disclose unavoidable conflicts.
5. Be vigilant and courageous about holding those with power accountable.
6. Deny favored treatment to advertisers and special interests and resist their pressure to influence news coverage.
7. Be wary of sources offering information for favors or money; avoid bidding for news.

Be Accountable

Journalists are accountable to their readers, listeners, viewers and each other. Journalists should:

1. Clarify and explain news coverage and invite dialogue with the public over journalistic conduct.
2. Encourage the public to voice grievances against the news media.
3. Admit mistakes and correct them promptly.
4. Expose unethical practices of journalists and the news media.
5. Abide by the same high standards to which they hold others.

The SPJ Code of Ethics is voluntarily embraced by thousands of journalists, regardless of place or platform, and is widely used in newsrooms and classrooms as a guide for ethical behavior. The code is intended not as a set of "rules" but as a resource for ethical decision-making. It is not — nor can it be under the First Amendment — legally enforceable.

Radio Television Digital News Association Code of Ethics

Preamble

Professional electronic journalists should operate as trustees of the public, seek the truth, report it fairly and with integrity and independence, and stand accountable for their actions.

Public Trust

Professional electronic journalists should recognize that their first obligation is to the public. Professional electronic journalists should:

1. Understand that any commitment other than service to the public undermines trust and credibility.
2. Recognize that service in the public interest creates an obligation to reflect the diversity of the community and guard against oversimplification of issues or events.
3. Provide a full range of information to enable the public to make enlightened decisions.
4. Fight to ensure that the public's business is conducted in public.

Truth

Professional electronic journalists should pursue truth aggressively and present the news accurately, in context, and as completely as possible. Professional electronic journalists should:

1. Continuously seek the truth.
2. Resist distortions that obscure the importance of events.
3.Clearly disclose the origin of information and label all material provided by outsiders.

Professional electronic journalists should not:

1. Report anything known to be false.
2. Manipulate images or sounds in any way that is misleading.
3. Plagiarize.
4. Present images or sounds that are reenacted without informing the public.

Fairness

Professional electronic journalists should present the news fairly and impartially, placing primary value on significance and relevance. Professional electronic journalists should:

1. Treat all subjects of news coverage with respect and dignity, showing particular compassion to victims of crime or tragedy.
2. Exercise special care when children are involved in a story and give children greater privacy protection than adults.

3. Seek to understand the diversity of their community and inform the public without bias or stereotype.
4. Present a diversity of expressions, opinions, and ideas in context.
5. Present analytical reporting based on professional perspective, not personal bias.
6. Respect the right to a fair trial.

Integrity

Professional electronic journalists should present the news with integrity and decency, avoiding real or perceived conflicts of interest, and respect the dignity and intelligence of the audience as well as the subjects of news. Professional electronic journalists should:

1. Identify sources whenever possible. Confidential sources should be used only when it is clearly in the public interest to gather or convey important information or when a person providing information might be harmed. Journalists should keep all commitments to protect a confidential source.
2. Clearly label opinion and commentary.
3. Guard against extended coverage of events or individuals that fails to significantly advance a story, place the event in context, or add to the public knowledge.
4. Refrain from contacting participants in violent situations while the situation is in progress.

5. Use technological tools with skill and thoughtfulness, avoiding techniques that skew facts, distort reality, or sensationalize events.
6. Use surreptitious newsgathering techniques, including hidden cameras or microphones, only if there is no other way to obtain stories of significant public importance and only if the technique is explained to the audience.
7. Disseminate the private transmissions of other news organizations only with permission.

Professional electronic journalists should not:

1. Pay news sources who have a vested interest in a story.
2. Accept gifts, favors, or compensation from those who might seek to influence coverage.
3. Engage in activities that may compromise their integrity or independence.

Independence

Professional electronic journalists should defend the independence of all journalists from those seeking influence or control over news content. Professional electronic journalists should:

1. Gather and report news without fear or favor, and vigorously resist undue influence from any outside forces, including advertisers, sources, story subjects, powerful individuals, and special interest groups.
2. Resist those who would seek to buy or politically influence news content or who would

seek to intimidate those who gather and disseminate the news.

3. Determine news content solely through editorial judgment and not as the result of outside influence.

4. Resist any self-interest or peer pressure that might erode journalistic duty and service to the public.

5. Recognize that sponsorship of the news will not be used in any way to determine, restrict, or manipulate content.

6. Refuse to allow the interests of ownership or management to influence news judgment and content inappropriately.

7. Defend the rights of the free press for all journalists, recognizing that any professional or government licensing of journalists is a violation of that freedom.

Accountability

Professional electronic journalists should recognize that they are accountable for their actions to the public, the profession, and themselves. Professional electronic journalists should:

1. Actively encourage adherence to these standards by all journalists and their employers.

2. Respond to public concerns. Investigate complaints and correct errors promptly and with as much prominence as the original report.

3. Explain journalistic processes to the public, especially when practices spark questions or controversy.

4. Recognize that professional electronic journalists are duty-bound to conduct themselves ethically.

5. Refrain from ordering or encouraging courses of action that would force employees to commit an unethical act.

6. Carefully listen to employees who raise ethical objections and create environments in which such objections and discussions are encouraged.

7. Seek support for and provide opportunities to train employees in ethical decision-making.

American Society of Newspaper Editors Statement of Principles

Preamble

The First Amendment, protecting freedom of expression from abridgment by any law, guarantees to the people through their press a constitutional right, and thereby places on news people a particular responsibility. Thus, journalism demands of its practitioners not only industry and knowledge but also the pursuit of a standard of integrity proportionate to the journalist's singular obligation. To this end the American Society of News Editors sets forth this Statement of Principles as a standard encouraging the highest ethical and professional performance.

Article I- Responsibility

The primary purpose of gathering and distributing news and opinion is to serve the general welfare by informing the people and enabling them to make judgments on the issues of the time. Newsmen and women who abuse the power of their professional role for selfish motives or unworthy purposes are faithless to that public trust. The American press was made free not just to inform or just to serve as a forum for debate but also to bring an independent scrutiny to bear on the forces of power in the society, including the conduct of official power at all levels of government.

Article II - Freedom of the Press

Freedom of the press belongs to the people. It must be defended against encroachment or assault from any quarter, public or private. Journalists must be constantly alert to see that the public's business is conducted in public. They must be vigilant against all who would exploit the press for selfish purposes.

Article III - Independence

Journalists must avoid impropriety and the appearance of impropriety as well as any conflict of interest or the appearance of conflict. They should neither accept anything nor pursue any activity that might compromise or seem to compromise their integrity.

Article IV - Truth and Accuracy

Good faith with the reader is the foundation of good journalism. Every effort must be made to assure that the news content is accurate, free from bias and in context, and that all sides are presented fairly. Editorials, analytical articles and commentary should be held to the same standards of accuracy with respect to facts as news reports. Significant errors of fact, as well as errors of omission, should be corrected promptly and prominently

Article V - Impartiality

To be impartial does not require the press to be unquestioning or to refrain from editorial expression. Sound practice, however, demands a clear distinction for the reader between news reports and opinion. Articles that contain opinion or personal interpretation should be clearly identified.

Article VI - Fair Play

Journalists should respect the rights of people involved in the news, observe the common standards of decency and stand accountable to the public for the fairness and accuracy of their news reports. Persons publicly accused should be given the earliest opportunity to respond. Pledges of confidentiality to news sources must be honored at all costs, and therefore should not be given lightly. Unless there is clear and pressing need to maintain confidences, sources of information should be identified.

These principles are intended to preserve, protect and strengthen the bond of trust and respect between American journalists and the American people, a bond that is essential to sustain the grant of freedom entrusted to both by the nation's founders.

Public Relations Society of America Code of Ethics

Preamble

This Code applies to PRSA members. The Code is designed to be a useful guide for PRSA members as they carry out their ethical responsibilities. This document is designed to anticipate and accommodate, by precedent, ethical challenges that may arise. The scenarios outlined in the Code provision are actual examples of misconduct. More will be added as experience with the Code occurs.

The Public Relations Society of America (PRSA) is committed to ethical practices. The level of public trust PRSA members seek, as we serve the public good, means we have taken on a special obligation to operate ethically.

The value of member reputation depends upon the ethical conduct of everyone affiliated with the Public Relations Society of America. Each of us sets an example for each other - as well as other professionals - by our pursuit of excellence with powerful standards of performance, professionalism, and ethical conduct.

Emphasis on enforcement of the Code has been eliminated. But, the PRSA Board of Directors retains the right to bar from membership or expel from the Society any individual who has been or is sanctioned by a government agency or convicted in a court of law of an action that is not in compliance with the Code.

Ethical practice is the most important obligation of a PRSA member. We view the Member Code of Ethics as a model for other professions, organizations, and professionals.

PRSA Member Statement of Professional Values

This statement presents the core values of PRSA members and, more broadly, of the public relations profession. These values provide the foundation for the Member Code of Ethics and set the industry standard for the professional practice of public relations. These values are the fundamental beliefs that guide our behaviors and decision-making process. We believe our professional values are vital to the integrity of the profession as a whole.

Advocacy

We serve the public interest by acting as responsible advocates for those we represent. We provide a voice in the marketplace of ideas, facts, and viewpoints to aid informed public debate.

Honesty

We adhere to the highest standards of accuracy and truth in advancing the interests of those we represent and in communicating with the public.

Expertise

We acquire and responsibly use specialized knowledge and experience. We advance the profession through continued professional development, research, and education. We build mutual understanding, credibility, and relationships among a wide array of institutions and audiences.

Independence

We provide objective counsel to those we represent. We are accountable for our actions.

Loyalty

We are faithful to those we represent, while honoring our obligation to serve the public interest.

Fairness

We deal fairly with clients, employers, competitors, peers, vendors, the media, and the general public. We respect all opinions and support the right of free expression.

PRSA Code Provisions

Free Flow of Information

Core Principle: Protecting and advancing the free flow of accurate and truthful information is essential to serving the public interest and contributing to informed decision making in a democratic society.

Intent: To maintain the integrity of relationships with the media, government officials, and the public.

To aid informed decision-making.

Guidelines: A member shall:

1. Preserve the integrity of the process of communication.
2. Be honest and accurate in all communications.
3. Act promptly to correct erroneous communications for which the practitioner is responsible.
4. Preserve the free flow of unprejudiced information when giving or receiving gifts by ensuring that gifts are nominal, legal, and infrequent.

Examples of Improper Conduct Under this Provision:

1. A member representing a ski manufacturer gives a pair of expensive racing skis to a sports magazine columnist, to influence the columnist to write favorable articles about the product.
2. A member entertains a government official beyond legal limits and/or in violation of government reporting requirements.

Competition

Core Principle: Promoting healthy and fair competition among professionals preserves an ethical climate while fostering a robust business environment.

Intent:

1. To promote respect and fair competition among public relations professionals.

2. To serve the public interest by providing the widest choice of practitioner options.

Guidelines: A member shall:

1. Follow ethical hiring practices designed to respect free and open competition without deliberately undermining a competitor.
2. Preserve intellectual property rights in the marketplace.

Examples of Improper Conduct Under This Provision:

1. A member employed by a "client organization" shares helpful information with a counseling firm that is competing with others for the organization's business.
2. A member spreads malicious and unfounded rumors about a competitor in order to alienate the competitor's clients and employees in a ploy to recruit people and business.

Disclosure of Information

Core Principle: Open communication fosters informed decision making in a democratic society.

Intent: To build trust with the public by revealing all information needed for responsible decision making.

Guidelines: A member shall:

1. Be honest and accurate in all communications.

2. Act promptly to correct erroneous communications for which the member is responsible.

3. Investigate the truthfulness and accuracy of information released on behalf of those represented.

4. Reveal the sponsors for causes and interests represented.

5. Disclose financial interest (such as stock ownership) in a client's organization.

6. Avoid deceptive practices.

Examples of Improper Conduct Under this Provision:

1. Front groups: A member implements "grass roots" campaigns or letter-writing campaigns to legislators on behalf of undisclosed interest groups.

2. Lying by omission: A practitioner for a corporation knowingly fails to release financial information, giving a misleading impression of the corporation's performance.

3. A member discovers inaccurate information disseminated via a website or media kit and does not correct the information.

4. A member deceives the public by employing people to pose as volunteers to speak at public hearings and participate in "grass roots" campaigns.

Safeguarding Confidences

Core Principle: Client trust requires appropriate protection of confidential and private information.

Intent: To protect the privacy rights of clients, organizations, and individuals by safeguarding confidential information.

Guidelines: A member shall:

1. Safeguard the confidences and privacy rights of present, former, and prospective clients and employees.
2. Protect privileged, confidential, or insider information gained from a client or organization.
3. Immediately advise an appropriate authority if a member discovers that confidential information is being divulged by an employee of a client company or organization.

Examples of Improper Conduct Under This Provision:

1. A member changes jobs, takes confidential information, and uses that information in the new position to the detriment of the former employer.
2. A member intentionally leaks proprietary information to the detriment of some other party.

Conflicts of Interest

Core Principle: Avoiding real, potential or perceived conflicts of interest builds the trust of clients, employers, and the publics.

Intent:

1. To earn trust and mutual respect with clients or employers.

2. To build trust with the public by avoiding or ending situations that put one's personal or professional interests in conflict with society's interests.

Guidelines: A member shall:

1. Act in the best interests of the client or employer, even subordinating the member's personal interests.
2. Avoid actions and circumstances that may appear to compromise good business judgment or create a conflict between personal and professional interests.
3. Disclose promptly any existing or potential conflict of interest to affected clients or organizations.
4. Encourage clients and customers to determine if a conflict exists after notifying all affected parties.

Examples of Improper Conduct Under This Provision:

1. The member fails to disclose that he or she has a strong financial interest in a client's chief competitor.
2. The member represents a "competitor company" or a "conflicting interest" without informing a prospective client.

Enhancing the Profession

Core Principle: Public relations professionals work constantly to strengthen the public's trust in the profession.

Intent:

1. To build respect and credibility with the public for the profession of public relations.
2. To improve, adapt and expand professional practices.

Guidelines: A member shall:

1. Acknowledge that there is an obligation to protect and enhance the profession.
2. Keep informed and educated about practices in the profession to ensure ethical conduct.
3. Actively pursue personal professional development.
4. Decline representation of clients or organizations that urge or require actions contrary to this Code.
5. Accurately define what public relations activities can accomplish.
6. Counsel subordinates in proper ethical decision making.
7. Require that subordinates adhere to the ethical requirements of the Code.
8. Report practices not in compliance with the Code, whether committed by PRSA members or not, to the appropriate authority.

Examples of Improper Conduct Under This Provision:

1. A PRSA member declares publicly that a product the client sells is safe, without disclosing evidence to the contrary.

2. A member initially assigns some questionable client work to a non-member practitioner to avoid the ethical obligation of PRSA membership.

PRSA Member Code of Ethics Pledge

I pledge: To conduct myself professionally, with truth, accuracy, fairness, and responsibility to the public; To improve my individual competence and advance the knowledge and proficiency of the profession through continuing research and education; And to adhere to the articles of the Member Code of Ethics 2000 for the practice of public relations as adopted by the governing Assembly of the Public Relations Society of America. I understand and accept that there is a consequence for misconduct, up to and including membership revocation. And, I understand that those who have been or are sanctioned by a government agency or convicted in a court of law of an action that is not in compliance with the Code may be barred from membership or expelled from the Society.

National Press Photographers Association

Preamble

The National Press Photographers Association, a professional society that promotes the highest standards in visual journalism, acknowledges concern for every person's need both to be fully informed about public events and to be recognized as part of the world in which we live.

Visual journalists operate as trustees of the public. Our primary role is to report visually on the significant events and varied viewpoints in our common world. Our primary goal is the faithful and comprehensive depiction of the subject at hand. As visual journalists, we have the responsibility to document society and to preserve its history through images. Photographic and video images can reveal great truths, expose wrongdoing and neglect, inspire hope and understanding and connect people around the globe through the language of visual understanding. Photographs can also cause great harm if they are callously intrusive or are manipulated.

This code is intended to promote the highest quality in all forms of visual journalism and to strengthen public confidence in the profession. It is also meant to serve as an educational tool both for those who practice and for those who appreciate photojournalism. To that end,

The National Press Photographers Association sets forth the following.

Code of Ethics

Visual journalists and those who manage visual news productions are accountable for upholding the following standards in their daily work:

1. Be accurate and comprehensive in the representation of subjects.
2. Resist being manipulated by staged photo opportunities.
3. Be complete and provide context when photographing or recording subjects. Avoid stereotyping individuals and groups. Recognize and work to avoid presenting one's own biases in the work.
4. Treat all subjects with respect and dignity. Give special consideration to vulnerable subjects and compassion to victims of crime or tragedy. Intrude on private moments of grief only when the public has an overriding and justifiable need to see.
5. While photographing subjects do not intentionally contribute to, alter, or seek to alter or influence events.
6. Editing should maintain the integrity of the photographic images' content and context. Do not manipulate images or add or alter sound in any way that can mislead viewers or misrepresent subjects.
7. Do not pay sources or subjects or reward them materially for information or participation.

8. Do not accept gifts, favors, or compensation from those who might seek to influence coverage.
9. Do not intentionally sabotage the efforts of other journalists.

Ideally, visual journalists should:

1. Strive to ensure that the public's business is conducted in public. Defend the rights of access for all journalists.
2. Think proactively, as a student of psychology, sociology, politics and art to develop a unique vision and presentation. Work with a voracious appetite for current events and contemporary visual media.
3. Strive for total and unrestricted access to subjects, recommend alternatives to shallow or rushed opportunities, seek a diversity of viewpoints, and work to show unpopular or unnoticed points of view.
4. Avoid political, civic and business involvements or other employment that compromise or give the appearance of compromising one's own journalistic independence.
5. Strive to be unobtrusive and humble in dealing with subjects.
6. Respect the integrity of the photographic moment.
7. Strive by example and influence to maintain the spirit and high standards expressed in this code.

When confronted with situations in which the proper action is not clear, seek the counsel of those who exhibit the highest standards of the profession. Visual journalists should continuously study their craft and the ethics that guide it.

Ethics & Social Media at NPR

The Internet and the social media communities it encompasses can be incredible resources. They offer both a remarkably robust amount of historical material and an incredible amount of "real-time" reporting from people at the scenes of breaking news events. But they also present new and unfamiliar challenges, and they tend to amplify the effects of any ethical misjudgments you might make. So, tread carefully. Conduct yourself online just as you would in any other public circumstances as an NPR journalist. Treat those you encounter online with fairness, honesty and respect, just as you would offline. Verify information before passing it along. Be honest about your intent when reporting. Avoid actions that might discredit your professional impartiality. And always remember, you represent NPR.

Accuracy

Guideline

Don't just spread information. Be careful and skeptical. When determining whether to pass along information being reported on social media sites by other news outlets or individuals, be thoughtful. When we point to what others are saying, in the eyes of many we are effectively reporting that information ourselves. This is true whether the platform is an official NPR social media webpage, a personal blog or a Twitter page that is written by an NPR journalist. But we also know that reporting about what's being posted on social media can give our listeners and readers valuable insights into the day's news.

One key is to be transparent about what we're doing. We tell readers what has and hasn't been confirmed. We challenge those putting information out on social media to provide evidence. We raise doubts and ask questions when we have concerns — sometimes "knocking down" rumors circulating on the Web is of enormous value to our readers. And we always ask an important question: am I about to spread a thinly-sourced rumor or am I passing on valuable and credible (even if unverified) information in a transparent manner with appropriate caveats?

Above all, proceed with caution, especially when news is breaking and accounts vary widely about what is happening. Reach out to other sources for confirmation. And the general standard is simple: Tweet and retweet as if what you're saying or passing along is information that you would put on the air or in a "traditional" NPR.org news story. If it needs context, attribution, clarification or "knocking down," provide it.

Guideline

When in doubt, consult the social media team. Of course, it's not always obvious how to apply journalistic principles to the social media arena. One resource always available to NPR journalists is our "social media team." Its members have expertise in collecting information from a variety of sources, in establishing to the best of their ability the credibility of those voices and the information they are posting, and in analyzing the material they use. Always make clear to listeners and readers what has been obtained from our original reporting and what we've found posted in social media outlets. And to the greatest practical extent, spell out how the information was checked and why we consider the sources credible. We may also invite our audience to assist in our efforts to monitor and verify what's being reported on social media. Such crowdsourcing does not determine what NPR journalists report, but it does add to our knowledge. The team can be reached via email (look for SocialMedia in the NPR internal email address book).

Guideline

Follow up offline when appropriate. It's often easier to falsify one's identity online than it is in the offline world. And tonal or contextual nuances can be lost in online exchanges. So, when appropriate, clarify and confirm information collected online through phone and in-person interviews. For example, when a social media posting is itself news, try to contact the source to confirm the origin of the information and attain a better understanding of its meaning. We must try to be as sophisticated in our use of social media as our audience and users are. The social media team is a key asset in this effort.

Guideline

Take care in using images that have been posted online. Increasingly, photos and video are being posted online by individuals. In considering whether to use those materials, do your best to verify their accuracy and when in doubt, do not publish them.

Images can be manipulated. Old video can be reposted and made to appear as if it's new. Photos or video taken in one part of the world can be repackaged and portrayed as being from somewhere else. Again, when in doubt, leave them out. As with all information, bring a healthy skepticism to images you encounter, starting from the assumption that all such images or video are not authentic. Then, with guidance from NPR's multimedia and social media teams (and if legal issues are involved, NPR's legal team as well), work through a series of questions, including:

1.When was it posted?
2.Do the images or video match what has been distributed by professionals (wire services, news networks, etc.)?
3.Is it original work or copies of what others have done?
4.Does this person have the legal right to distribute the work and has he made the materials available for others to use?

Honesty

Just as we do in the "real" world, we identify ourselves as NPR journalists when we are working online. So, if as part of our work we are posting comments, asking questions, tweeting, retweeting, blogging, Facebooking or doing anything on social media or other online forums, we clearly identify ourselves and that we work for NPR. We do not use pseudonyms when doing such work.

NPR journalists may, in the course of their work, "follow" or "friend" Twitter accounts, Facebook pages and other social media sites created by political parties and advocacy groups. But we do so to monitor their news feeds, not to become participants, and we follow and friend sites created by advocates from all sides of the issues. It's as basic a tool as signing up to be on mailing lists used to be.

If in their personal lives NPR journalists join online forums and social media sites, they may follow the conventions of those outlets and use screen names that do not identify who they are. But we do not use information gathered from our interactions on such sites in our reports for NPR. If we get ideas for stories, we treat the information just as we would anything we see in the "real world" — as a starting point that needs to be followed by open, honest reporting.

Finally, we acknowledge that nothing on the Web is truly private. Even on purely recreational or cultural sites and even if what we're doing is personal and not identified as coming from someone at NPR, we understand that what we say and do could still reflect on NPR. So, we do nothing that could undermine our credibility with the public, damage NPR's standing as an impartial source of news, or otherwise jeopardize NPR's reputation. In other words, we don't behave any differently than we would in any public setting or on an NPR broadcast.

Case Studies

There is no privacy on the Web.

Imagine, if you will, an NPR legal correspondent named Sue Zemencourt. She's a huge fan of Enormous University's basketball team and loves to chat online about EU. She posts comments on blogs under the screen name "enormous1." One day, an equally rabid fan of Gigormous State ("gigormous1") posts obnoxious comments about EU.

Sue snaps. Expletives and insults fly from her fingers on to the webpage. They're so out-of-line that the blog blocks her from submitting any more comments — and discovers that her i.p. address leads back to NPR. The blog's host posts that "someone at NPR is using language that the FCC definitely would not approve of" and describes what was said. Things go viral.

The basically good person that she is, Sue publicly acknowledges and apologizes for her mistake. But that doesn't stop The Daily Show from satirizing about the "NPRNormous Explosion."

Damage done.

Be circumspect about your behavior, even when the exchange feels private or anonymous. Even an email to a trusted recipient can be made public, with or without the recipient's knowledge or consent.

Guideline

Online sources should be on-the-record too. In today's world, many contacts with sources are made online — via emails and social media sites. As we discuss in the guidelines about accuracy and transparency, NPR pushes to keep its interviews on-the-record. The same is true of our "virtual" interactions with sources. We make that clear to potential sources when we reach out to them.

Independence

Guideline

When posting or gathering material online, consider terms of service. It's important to keep in mind that the terms of service of a social media site apply to what we post there and to the information we gather from it. Also: The terms might allow for our material to be used in a different way than intended. Additionally, law enforcement officials may be able to obtain our reporting on these sites by subpoena without our consent — or perhaps even our knowledge. Social media is a vital reporting resource for us, but we must be vigilant about keeping work that may be sensitive in our own hands.

Impartiality

Guideline

Our standards of impartiality also apply to social media. Refrain from advocating for political or other polarizing issues online. This extends to joining online groups or using social media in any form (including your Facebook page or a personal blog). Don't express personal views on a political or other controversial issue that you could not write for the air or post on NPR.org. These guidelines apply whether you are posting under your own name or — if the online site allows pseudonyms — your identity would not be readily apparent. In reality, anything you post online reflects both on you and on NPR.

Your simple participation in some online groups could be seen to indicate that you endorse their views. Consider whether you can accomplish your purposes by just observing a group's activity, rather than becoming a member. If you do join, be clear that you've done so to seek information or story ideas. And if you "friend" or join a group representing one side of an issue, do so for groups representing other viewpoints.

Accountability

Guideline

Social media outlets are public spaces. We know that everything we write or receive on a social media site is public. Anyone with access to the Web can potentially see what we're doing. And regardless of how careful we are in trying to keep them separate, our professional lives and our personal lives overlap when we're online.

The line between private and public activity has been blurred by these tools. Information from a Facebook page, blog entries, and tweets — even if they're intended to be personal messages to friends or family — can be easily circulated beyond the intended audiences. The content, therefore, represents us and NPR to the outside world — as do our radio pieces and stories for NPR.org. This applies to the people and organizations we choose to "friend" or "like" online as well. Those are content choices as much as a message or blog post. As in all of all reporting, the NPR Guiding Principles guide our use of social media.

Rule of thumb: You should conduct yourself in social media forums with an eye to how your behavior or comments might appear if we were called upon to defend them as a news organization. In other words, don't behave any differently online than you would in any other public setting.

And a final caution – when in doubt, consult with your supervisor.

Case Studies & Key Questions

Can we follow political parties or advocacy groups related to our beats? If your work includes coverage of politics and social issues, can you "follow" or "friend" a political party or advocacy group?

Yes, if you're doing it to keep up on what that party or group is doing. And you should be following those on the other side of the issues as well.

Guideline

Self-protection is part of being accountable online. Protect yourself: Use the highest level of privacy tools available to control access to your personal activity when appropriate, but don't let that make you complacent. It's just not that hard for someone to bypass those safeguards and make public what you thought was private.

Don't be careless. Keep your opinions to yourself. Imagine what you say or write landing in an AP story or in The Washington Post, and imagine the damage that could cause you or NPR.

Guideline

Consider the legal implications of your actions, regardless of the medium.

Whether in an NPR newscast or a tweet, "you always have to take into consideration what you're saying, what you know, what you don't know, and be thoughtful about not making libelous comments whatever the medium." (Source: NPR's Ashley Messenger, in an article on Poynter.org.

In many cases, a journalist will be legally responsible for any statement he or she repeats, even if the statement is attributed to another source. There are a few exceptions, and one of them is Section 230 of the

Communications Decency Act, which protects news organizations from defamation liability for content that's created by a third party. Many experts believe this protection would extend to retweets. Citizen Media Law Project co-founder David Ardia put it this way in a Poynter.org story: "So if a journalist or news organization were to retweet a defamatory statement, they would not be held accountable. If, however, they added a defamatory remark as part of the retweet, they could be."

So, in theory NPR would be protected if someone retweets a post that says something defamatory or inaccurate about someone. But be careful about adding comments that would make the message your own and destroy immunity.

But beyond the legal implications, it is important to consider our listeners and readers and the fact that they trust that the information we're giving them is as accurate as we can make it. This extends to the information we tweet, retweet, blog, tumble or share in any other way on social media. And that's why we don't simply pass along information — even via something as seemingly innocent as a retweet — if we doubt the credibility of the source or news outlet. We push for confirmation. We look for other sources. We reach out to those closer to the story. In other words, we do some reporting.

Respect

Guideline

Be considerate of community norms.

Realize that different communities – online and offline – have their own culture, etiquette, and norms, and be respectful of them. Our ethics don't change in different circumstances, but our decisions might.

The foundation of respect in reporting on any community is awareness. Strive to be knowledgeable about the culture, and be attuned to gaps in your understanding. Often your colleagues can be a terrific resource to help you get up to speed on unfamiliar settings.

Consider as well how your conduct in a community will affect your reporting. As you adjust behaviors such as language and dress in different situations, think about what might be most helpful or harmful to effective reporting.

Also, appreciate that journalism can be an intrusive act, and conduct yourself as a decent guest of the community where you're reporting. If the customary etiquette is to remove your shoes upon entering a building, for example, it's appropriate to oblige.

And of course, factor in your own security. In unstable situations, for example, journalists can be targets of violence. At such times, the most appropriate consideration may merely be blending in. As always, we rely on your good judgment.

Guideline

Respect NPR's copyright.

While we strongly encourage linking to NPR.org, you may not repost NPR copyrighted material to social networks without prior permission. For example, it is o.k. to link from your blog or Facebook profile to a story of yours on the NPR site, but you should not copy the full text or audio onto a personal site or Web page. You may accomplish this through the NPR API or widgets that NPR provides to the public. Assume the terms of use that apply to the public also apply to your usage in these situations.

Excellence

Guideline

Social media are excellent tools when handled correctly. Social networking sites, such as Facebook and Twitter have become an integral part of everyday life for millions of people around the world. As NPR grows to serve an audience that extends well beyond radio listeners, social media are becoming an increasingly important aspect of how we interact with our audiences. Properly used, social networking sites can be valuable parts of our newsgathering and reporting kits because they can speed research and quickly extend a reporter's contacts. They are also useful transparency tools — allowing us to open up our reporting and editing processes when appropriate. We encourage our journalists to take advantage of them.

But reporting in social media spaces requires the same diligence we exercise when reporting in other environments. When NPR bloggers post about breaking news, they do not cite anonymous posts on social media sites — though they may use information they find there to guide their reporting. They carefully attribute the information they cite and are clear about what NPR has and has not been able to confirm.

When NPR correspondents go on the air they may mention discussions they've seen on social media sites as reflecting in part the tone or mood or general reaction to an event. But they realize that is not the same as a scientific survey of public opinion or a substitute for the kind of in-depth reporting that leads to a deep understanding of a subject.

And all NPR journalists understand that to get the most out of social media we need to understand those communities. So, we respect their cultures and treat those we encounter online with the same courtesy and understanding as anyone we deal with in the offline world. We do not impose ourselves on such sites. We are guests and behave as such.

Insights Association Code of Standards and Ethics for Market Research and Data Analytics

PREFACE

The Insights Association is the U.S. association representing companies, corporate research and data analytics departments, and individuals working in the marketing, opinion and social research and data analytics industry and profession. The Insights Association was founded in 2017 with the merger of CASRO, a trade association formed in 1975, and MRA, a professional society founded in 1957. The Insights Association, established to foster and promote the interests of the U.S. industry and profession, serves organizations and their research-related employees including data scientists, as well as individual research professionals not affiliated with member organizations. The Association's members may include research companies and their employees, corporate research departments and their employees, data scientists generating data analytics, organizations and individuals supporting research activities, universities, educators and students, as well as others.

The Insights Association's mission is to provide the environment and leadership that will advance the integrity, quality, and best interests of the U.S. industry and profession. The Association supports standards, guidelines, education and information resources, and self-regulation in research process, practice, and performance.

The Insights Association also works closely with other national and international associations to support and improve the integrity and quality of marketing research and data analytics across geographic and cultural borders.

The Insights Association Code of Standards and Ethics (the "Code") is based on the codes of both CASRO and MRA. The Code also draws on the ICC/ESOMAR Code and the codes of other national research associations, embracing and affirming principles common to them.

PURPOSE

This Code presents the fundamental, overarching principles of ethics and professionalism for the industry. Its purpose is to promote the importance and value of the work undertaken by Insights Association members and promote the interests of the industry and profession to the constituencies that they serve. Further, the Code seeks to establish a platform for self-regulation, building on the successful efforts of CASRO and MRA, to foster confidence in the industry and profession and ensure its continued success.

The Code is supplemented by guidelines that assist practitioners and companies with its application.

The inclusion of data analytics in the Code recognizes changes in the industry and profession and the proliferation of data that has resulted in a changing role for members and the services they provide. The Code recognizes the global nature of the industry and profession and the requirement to comply with all applicable state, national and international laws and regulations.

INTERPRETATION

This Code sets the standards of professional and ethical conduct for all Insights Association members and the marketing research and data analytics industry and profession.

In the event of a conflict between this Code and applicable law, applicable law shall govern. This Code is to be interpreted in conjunction with other relevant guidelines and principles. These and other supplemental documents are referenced at the end of this document.

The Code has been organized into sections describing the responsibilities of members. The

Code is not intended to be, nor is it, an immutable document. Circumstances may arise that are not covered or that may call for modification. The Code, therefore, seeks to be responsive to the changes in marketing research and data analytics. The Standards Committee and Board of Directors of the Insights Association will evaluate these changes and, if appropriate, revise the Code.

Adherence to the Code is required by all members of the Insights Association. The Insights Association requires its members to review and attest to this Code as part of their membership application and annual membership renewal. In so doing, members grant the Insights Association the authority to enforce the Code and will cooperate with the Association's enforcement efforts. Information regarding enforcement may be found in the Enforcement section at the end of this document. The Association's Standards Committee is available to address any complaints and alleged breaches of the Code.

Throughout this document, the word "must" is used to identify mandatory requirements, a principle or practice that researchers are obliged to follow. The word "should" indicates a recommended practice.

Definitions

For the purposes of the Code, the following terms have these specific meanings:

Children – Individuals for whom consent to participate in research must be obtained from a parent or legal guardian. Definitions of the age of a child vary substantially and are set by national laws and self-regulatory codes. In the U.S., a child is defined as being age 12 and under. In the absence of a national definition, a child is defined as being age 12 and under and a "young person" as age 13 to 17.

Client – Any individual, organization, department or division, internal or external that requests, commissions or subscribes to all or any part of a research project.

Consent – Voluntary and informed agreement by a person for participation in research and/or the collection and processing of their personally identifiable information PII. This consent is based upon the data subject having been provided with clear information about the nature and purpose of the data being collected or used, with whom it will be shared and how it will be used. Depending on applicable law and regulation, particularly with consent for children or other vulnerable individuals, such consent may need to be verifiable.

Corporate researcher – An individual or department in a company or organization that commissions or carries out research or acts as a consultant on research that is for internal use by that company or organization.

Data analytics – The process of examining data sets to uncover hidden patterns, unknown correlations, trends, preferences and other useful information for research purposes. Data analytics also includes data integration, which is the process of integrating data from different sources.

Data subject – Anyone from whom data, which may include PII, are collected or used for research purposes. In cases where the data subject actively engages in research, a data subject may also be referred to as a research participant.

Non-research activity – Taking direct action toward an individual whose data, which may include PII, was collected or analyzed with the intent to change the attitudes, opinions or actions of that individual. Non-research activities include but are not limited to advertising, direct marketing and automated decision-making.

Passive data collection – The collection of data by observing, measuring, or recording a data subject's actions or behavior.

Personally identifiable information or PII (referred to as personal data in the EU and other jurisdictions) – Information that can be used to distinguish or trace the identity of an individual, either alone or when combined with other personal or identifying information. PII can include information such as name, social security number, date and place of birth, mother's maiden name, biometric records, photographs, sound or video recording, and other information that is linked or linkable to an individual, such as medical, educational, financial, and employment information.

Privacy policy (sometimes referred to as privacy notice) – A published summary of an organization's privacy practices describing the ways an organization gathers, uses, discloses and manages data subject's PII.

Primary data – Data collected from or about a data subject for the purpose of research.

Research – All forms of marketing, opinion and social research and data analytics used in the systematic gathering and interpretation of information about individuals and organizations. It uses the statistical and analytical methods and techniques of the applied social, behavioral and data sciences to generate insights and support decision-making by providers of goods and services, governments, non-profit organizations and the general public.

Researcher – Any individual or organization carrying out or acting as a consultant on research, including those working in client or corporate research departments as well as any subcontractors used.

Secondary data – Data collected for another purpose and subsequently used in research.

Sensitive data – Specific types of PII that local laws require be protected from unauthorized access to safeguard the privacy or security of an individual or organization to the highest possible standards. The definitions of sensitive data vary by jurisdiction. In the U.S., sensitive data includes health data and financial data. In other jurisdictions, like the EU, sensitive includes racial or ethnic origin, health records, sexual orientation or sexual habits, criminal records, political opinions, trade association membership, religious or philosophical beliefs, location, financial information, and illegal behaviors such as regulated drugs or alcohol.

Subcontractor – A service provider executing any element of a research or data analytics project on behalf of another entity.

Vulnerable individuals (may also be referred to as vulnerable people or populations) – Individuals who may have limited capacity to make voluntary and informed decisions.

FUNDAMENTAL PRINCIPLES OF THE CODE

The Code is based on the following principles:

1. Respect the data subjects and their rights as specified by law or by this code.
2. Be transparent about the collection of PII, only collect PII with consent and ensure the confidentiality and security of PII.
3. Act with high standards of integrity, professionalism and transparency in all relationships and practices.
4. Comply with all applicable laws and regulations.

Section 1: Duty of Care

Researchers must:

1. Be honest, transparent, and straightforward in all interactions.
2. Respect the rights and well-being of data subjects and make all reasonable efforts to ensure that data subjects are not harmed, disadvantaged or harassed as a result of their participation in research.
3. Always distinguish between research and non-research activities so as to maintain public confidence in the integrity of research.
4. When engaging in non-research activities (for example, promotional or commercial activities directed at data subjects, including but not limited to advertising and direct marketing), do not permit any

direct action to be taken against an individual based on his or her participation in research.

Section 2: Primary Data Collection
Transparency, Notice and Choice

Researchers must:

1. Promptly identify themselves to data subjects so that the participants can easily verify researcher identity and credentials.
2. Clearly state the general purpose of the research as soon as methodologically possible.
3. Ensure that participation is voluntary and based on accurate information about the general purpose and nature of the research.
4. Respect the right of data subjects to refuse requests to participate in research.
5. Respect the right of those already engaged in research to terminate their participation or refuse requests for additional or other forms of research participation.
6. Upon request, permit data subjects to access, correct or update any PII held about them.

Consent

Researchers must:

1. Obtain the data subject's consent for research participation and the collection of PII or ensure that

consent was properly obtained by the owner of the data or sample source.

2. Inform data subjects if there are any activities that will involve re-contact. In such situations, the researcher must obtain the data subject's consent to share PII for re-contacting purposes. Re-contacting data subjects for quality control purposes does not require prior notification.

3. Allow data subjects to withdraw their consent at any time.

4. Obtain consent from the data subject prior to using his/her data in a manner that is materially different from what data subject has agreed.

Section 3: Passive Data Collection

Whenever possible, passive data collection must be based on the consent of the data subject. In such situations, researchers must provide clear and simple methods for data subjects to grant and retract their consent.

Where it is not possible to obtain consent, researchers must have legally permissible grounds to collect the data and must remove or obscure any identifying characteristics as soon as operationally possible.

Section 4: Use of Secondary Data

When using secondary data for research that includes PII, researchers must:

1. Ensure that the use is not incompatible with the purpose for which the data was originally collected.
2. Ensure that the data was not collected in violation of restrictions imposed by laws or regulations, through deception, or in ways that were not apparent to or reasonably understood or anticipated by the data subject.
3. Ensure that the intended use is compatible with the consent obtained when the data was collected.
4. Honor all data subject requests that their data not be used.
5. Ensure that use of the data will not result in any harm to data subjects.

Section 5: Data Protection and Privacy

Researchers must:

1. Have a privacy policy that is easily available (including being publicly available if appropriate) and clearly states their data protection and privacy obligations and practices.
2. Only share a data subject's PII with any third-party[1]:
a. With that data subject's consent; or
b. In limited situations that are in the interest of the data subject or the public. Such limited situations include, but are not limited to: adverse event reporting, health and safety, and situations pursuant to required legal process.
3. Ensure that all PII collected, received or processed by the researcher or any subcontractor or other

service provider is secured and protected against loss, unauthorized access, use, modification, destruction or disclosure by the implementation of information security measures required by applicable laws and regulations.
4. Limit data collection to what is necessary for the specific research purposes.
5. When collecting PII for research that may also be used for non-research activities, inform data subjects of any non-research use prior to data collection and obtain their consent for any non-research activity.
6. Comply with all applicable international, national, state and local laws and regulations, and local codes of conduct with respect to PII and the local variations in the definition and requirements for sensitive data.

Section 6: Children and Vulnerable Individuals

Researchers must take special care when conducting research with children and other vulnerable individuals. When conducting a research project with such individuals, researchers must:

1. Obtain verifiable consent from a parent or legal guardian for children or other vulnerable individuals when required.
2. Take special care when considering whether to involve children and young people (minors) in research. The questions asked must take into account their age and level of maturity.

3. When working with other vulnerable individuals, researchers must ensure that such individuals are capable of making informed decisions and are not unduly pressured to cooperate in research.

Responsibilities to Clients

Section 7: Honesty and Transparency

Researchers must:

1. Be honest and transparent in all interactions.
2. Accurately represent their qualifications, skills, experience and resources.
3. Upon request, inform the client if any part of the work is subcontracted.
4. Inform all clients when a project is conducted on behalf of more than one client.
5. Not use any data collected solely for a specific client for any other purpose without permission.
6. Retain all data and research materials in compliance with applicable laws and regulations, industry quality standards, company processes or as requested by a specific client.
7. Work in good faith to resolve all disputes with clients.

Section 8: Research Quality

Researchers must:

1. Assist the client in designing effective research and clearly communicate any issues or limitations that may be associated with a chosen research design.
2. Perform all work in accordance with the specifications detailed in the research proposal or statement of work.
3. Perform all work in accordance with accepted methodological practices and principles. When new and emerging methodological practices are used, researchers must ensure that the underlying principles are methodologically sound.
4. Ensure that findings and interpretation are adequately supported by data and provide such supporting data to the client upon request.
5. Provide the technical information required to permit the client to verify that work meets contract specifications, while protecting PII (refer to Section 2: Primary Data Collection, Consent, #2 for more information).
6. Provide sufficient information to permit independent assessment of the quality of data presented and the validity of conclusions drawn.

Responsibilities to and of Corporate Researchers

Section 9: Corporate Researchers

Corporate researchers play multiple roles in the industry and profession. Depending on the specific situation, they may be clients, researchers, or both. Corporate researchers must always comply with all applicable requirements of this Code.

Responsibilities with Respect to Subcontracting

Section 10: Subcontracting

Researchers and subcontractors must:

1. Ensure that subcontractors are provided the appropriate level of information so that the researcher and the subcontractor can make an informed decision as to the subcontractor's suitability for participation.
2. Ensure that the parties do not have any conflicts of interest.
3. Ensure that the parties maintain the confidentiality and security of confidential and proprietary information, including PII, which was provided by either party.
4. Not use the confidential and proprietary information of either party, including PII, illegally or contrary to the agreement under which confidential or proprietary information was obtained.
5. Document all work and confidentiality requirements with written agreements that protect the interests of clients, researchers and subcontractors.

Responsibilities to the Public

Section 11: Research for Public Release

Researchers must:

1. Always obtain clear approval from clients to release findings publicly.
2. Ensure that the findings they release are an accurate portrayal of the research data, and that careful checks on the accuracy of all data presented are performed.
3. Provide the basic information, including technical details, to permit independent assessment of the quality and validity of the data presented and the conclusions drawn, unless prohibited by legitimate proprietary or contractual restrictions.
4. Make best efforts to ensure that they are consulted as to the form and content of publication when the client plans to publish the findings of a research project. Both the client and the researcher have a responsibility to ensure that published results are not misleading.
5. Not permit their name or that of their organization to be associated with the publishing of conclusions from a research project unless those conclusions are adequately supported by the data.
6. Promptly take appropriate actions to correct information if any public release is found to be incorrect.

LEGAL REQUIREMENTS

Section 12: Legal Requirements

Members must:

1. Comply with all applicable international, national, state and local laws and regulations, and local codes of conduct.
2. Not engage in any acts of bribery or induce any party to engage in illegal behavior.

Responsibilities to the Research Profession

Section 13: Professional Responsibility

Members must:

1. Comply with this Code.
2. Act with high standards of integrity, professionalism and transparency in all relationships and practices.
3. Engage in competitive practices that are reasonable in view of the interests of those competing and the public and do not include practices condemned by law as hostile to the public interest.

Enforcement

Enforcement of the Code is the responsibility of the Insights Association Standards Committee. Investigations into a Code violation may come as a result of a complaint that is filed or for any other reason deemed appropriate by the Insights Association. Investigations will include direct contact with the member involved in a Code violation complaint.

Investigations that find a failure to abide by this Code may result in sanctions ranging from the issuance of a private written warning to public expulsion from the Insights Association.

This Code will be reviewed annually by the Insights Association Standards Committee.

To file a complaint against a Member, please contact the Insights Association at enforcement@insightsassociation.org or (202) 800-2545.

AIGA Standards of professional practice

A professional designer adheres to principles of integrity that demonstrate respect for the profession, for colleagues, for clients, for audiences or consumers, and for society as a whole.

These standards define the expectations of a professional designer and represent the distinction of an AIGA member in the practice of design. AIGA members at the Supporter level and above who have agreed to adhere to these standards are denoted in the Designer Directory by an AIGA logo.

The designer's responsibility to clients

1.1 A professional designer shall acquaint himself or herself with a client's business and design standards and shall act in the client's best interest within the limits of professional responsibility.

1.2 A professional designer shall not work simultaneously on assignments that create a conflict of interest without agreement of the clients or employers concerned, except in specific cases where it is the convention of a particular trade for a designer to work at the same time for various competitors.

1.3 A professional designer shall treat all work in progress prior to the completion of a project and all knowledge of a client's intentions, production methods and business organization as confidential and shall not divulge such information in any manner whatsoever without the consent of the client. It is the designer's responsibility to ensure that all staff members act accordingly.

1.4 A professional designer who accepts instructions from a client or employer that involve violation of the designer's ethical standards should be corrected by the designer, or the designer should refuse the assignment.

The designer's responsibility to other designers

2.1 Designers in pursuit of business opportunities should support fair and open competition.

2.2 A professional designer shall not knowingly accept any professional assignment on which another designer has been or is working without notifying the other designer or until he or she is satisfied that any previous appointments have been properly terminated and that all materials relevant to the continuation of the project are the clear property of the client.

2.3 A professional designer must not attempt, directly or indirectly, to supplant or compete with another designer by means of unethical inducements.

2.4 A professional designer shall be objective and balanced in criticizing another designer's work and shall not denigrate the work or reputation of a fellow designer.

2.5 A professional designer shall not accept instructions from a client that involve infringement of another person's property rights without permission, or consciously act in any manner involving any such infringement.

2.6 A professional designer working in a country other than his or her own shall observe the relevant Code of Conduct of the national society concerned.

Fees

3.1 A professional designer shall work only for a fee, a royalty, salary or other agreed-upon form of compensation. A professional designer shall not retain any kickbacks, hidden discounts, commission, allowances or payment in kind from contractors or suppliers. Clients should be made aware of mark-ups.

3.2 A reasonable handling and administration charge may be added, with the knowledge and understanding of the client, as a percentage to all reimbursable items, billable to a client, that pass through the designer's account.

3.3 A professional designer who has a financial interest in any suppliers who may benefit from a recommendation made by the designer in the course of a project will inform the client or employer of this fact in advance of the recommendation.

3.4 A professional designer who is asked to advise on the selection of designers or the consultants shall not base such advice in the receipt of payment from the designer or consultants recommended.

Publicity

4.1 Any self-promotion, advertising or publicity must not contain deliberate misstatements of competence, experience or professional capabilities. It must be fair both to clients and other designers.

4.2 A professional designer may allow a client to use his or her name for the promotion of work designed or services provided in a manner that is appropriate to the status of the profession.

Authorship

5.1 A professional designer shall not claim sole credit for a design on which other designers have collaborated.

5.2 When not the sole author of a design, it is incumbent upon a professional designer to clearly identify his or her specific responsibilities or involvement with the design. Examples of such work may not be used for publicity, display or portfolio samples without clear identification of precise areas of authorship.

The designer's responsibility to the public

6.1 A professional designer shall avoid projects that will result in harm to the public.

6.2 A professional designer shall communicate the truth in all situations and at all times; his or her work shall not make false claims nor knowingly misinform. A professional designer shall represent messages in a clear manner in all forms of communication design and avoid false, misleading and deceptive promotion.

6.3 A professional designer shall respect the dignity of all audiences and shall value individual differences even as they avoid depicting or stereotyping people or groups of people in a negative or dehumanizing way. A professional designer shall strive to be sensitive to cultural values and beliefs and engages in fair and balanced communication design that fosters and encourages mutual understanding.

The designer's responsibility to society and the environment

7.1 A professional designer, while engaged in the practice or instruction of design, shall not knowingly do or fail to do anything that constitutes a deliberate or reckless disregard for the health and safety of the communities in which he or she lives and practices or the privacy of the individuals and businesses therein. A professional designer shall take a responsible role in the visual portrayal of people, the consumption of natural resources, and the protection of animals and the environment.

7.2 A professional designer is encouraged to contribute five percent of his or her time to projects in the public good-projects that serve society and improve the human experience.

7.3 A professional designer shall consider environmental, economic, social and cultural implications of his or her work and minimize the adverse impacts.

7.4 A professional designer shall not knowingly accept instructions from a client or employer that involve infringement of another person's or group's human rights or property rights without permission of such other person or group, or consciously act in any manner involving any such infringement.

7.5 A professional designer shall not knowingly make use of goods or services offered by manufacturers, suppliers or contractors that are accompanied by an obligation that is substantively detrimental to the best interests of his or her client, society or the environment.

7.6 A professional designer shall refuse to engage in or countenance discrimination on the basis of

race, sex, age, religion, national origin, sexual
orientation or disability.

7.7 A professional designer shall strive to
understand and support the principles of free
speech, freedom of assembly, and access to an open
marketplace of ideas and shall act accordingly.

The Constitution of the United States

The following is a transcription of the original Constitution as inscribed by Jacob Shallus on parchment (on display at the National Archives Museum). Spelling and punctuation reflect the original. *Reprinted from the National Archives webpage at archives.gov.*

We the People of the United States, in Order to form a more perfect Union, establish Justice, insure domestic Tranquility, provide for the common defense, promote the general Welfare, and secure the Blessings of Liberty to ourselves and our Posterity, do ordain and establish this Constitution for the United States of America.

Article. I.

Section. 1.

All legislative Powers herein granted shall be vested in a Congress of the United States, which shall consist of a Senate and House of Representatives.

Section. 2.

The House of Representatives shall be composed of Members chosen every second Year by the People of the several States, and the Electors in each State shall have the Qualifications requisite for Electors of the most numerous Branch of the State Legislature.

No Person shall be a Representative who shall not have attained to the Age of twenty-five Years, and been seven Years a Citizen of the United States, and who shall not, when elected, be an Inhabitant of that State in which he shall be chosen.

Representatives and direct Taxes shall be apportioned among the several States which may be included within this Union, according to their respective Numbers, which shall be determined by adding to the whole Number of free Persons, including those bound to Service for a Term of Years, and excluding Indians not taxed, three fifths of all other Persons. The actual Enumeration shall be made within three Years after the first Meeting of the Congress of the United States, and within every subsequent Term of ten Years, in such Manner as they shall by Law direct. The Number of Representatives shall not exceed one for every thirty Thousand, but each State shall have at Least one Representative; and until such enumeration shall be made, the State of New Hampshire shall be entitled to choose three, Massachusetts eight, Rhode-Island and Providence Plantations one, Connecticut five, New-York six, New Jersey four, Pennsylvania eight, Delaware one, Maryland six, Virginia ten, North Carolina five, South Carolina five, and Georgia three.

When vacancies happen in the Representation from any State, the Executive Authority thereof shall issue Writs of Election to fill such Vacancies.

The House of Representatives shall choose their Speaker and other Officers; and shall have the sole Power of Impeachment.

Section. 3.

The Senate of the United States shall be composed of two Senators from each State, chosen by the Legislature thereof, for six Years; and each Senator shall have one Vote.

Immediately after they shall be assembled in Consequence of the first Election, they shall be divided as equally as may be into three Classes. The Seats of the Senators of the first Class shall be vacated at the Expiration of the second Year, of the second Class at the Expiration of the fourth Year, and of the third Class at the Expiration of the sixth Year, so that one third may be chosen every second Year; and if Vacancies happen by Resignation, or otherwise, during the Recess of the Legislature of any State, the Executive thereof may make temporary Appointments until the next Meeting of the Legislature, which shall then fill such Vacancies.

No Person shall be a Senator who shall not have attained to the Age of thirty Years, and been nine Years a Citizen of the United States, and who shall not, when elected, be an Inhabitant of that State for which he shall be chosen.

The Vice President of the United States shall be President of the Senate, but shall have no Vote, unless they be equally divided.

The Senate shall choose their other Officers, and also a President pro tempore, in the Absence of the Vice President, or when he shall exercise the Office of President of the United States.

The Senate shall have the sole Power to try all Impeachments. When sitting for that Purpose, they shall be on Oath or Affirmation. When the President of the United States is tried, the Chief Justice shall preside: And no Person shall be convicted without the Concurrence of two thirds of the Members present.

Judgment in Cases of Impeachment shall not extend further than to removal from Office, and disqualification to hold and enjoy any Office of honor, Trust or Profit under the United States: but the Party convicted shall nevertheless be liable and subject to Indictment, Trial, Judgment and Punishment, according to Law.

Section. 4.

The Times, Places and Manner of holding Elections for Senators and Representatives, shall be prescribed in each State by the Legislature thereof; but the Congress may at any time by Law make or alter such Regulations, except as to the Places of choosing Senators.

The Congress shall assemble at least once in every Year, and such Meeting shall be on the first Monday in December, unless they shall by Law appoint a different Day.

Section. 5.

Each House shall be the Judge of the Elections, Returns and Qualifications of its own Members, and a Majority of each shall constitute a Quorum to do Business; but a smaller Number may adjourn from day to day, and may be authorized to compel the Attendance of absent Members, in such Manner, and under such Penalties as each House may provide.

Each House may determine the Rules of its Proceedings, punish its Members for disorderly Behavior, and, with the Concurrence of two thirds, expel a Member.

Each House shall keep a Journal of its Proceedings, and from time to time publish the same, excepting such Parts as may in their Judgment require Secrecy; and the Yeas and Nays of the Members of either House on any question shall, at the Desire of one fifth of those Present, be entered on the Journal.

Neither House, during the Session of Congress, shall, without the Consent of the other, adjourn for more than three days, nor to any other Place than that in which the two Houses shall be sitting.

Section. 6.

The Senators and Representatives shall receive a Compensation for their Services, to be ascertained by Law, and paid out of the Treasury of the United States. They shall in all Cases, except Treason, Felony and Breach of the Peace, be privileged from Arrest during their Attendance at the Session of their respective

Houses, and in going to and returning from the same; and for any Speech or Debate in either House, they shall not be questioned in any other Place.

No Senator or Representative shall, during the Time for which he was elected, be appointed to any civil Office under the Authority of the United States, which shall have been created, or the Emoluments whereof shall have been increased during such time; and no Person holding any Office under the United States, shall be a Member of either House during his Continuance in Office.

Section. 7.

All Bills for raising Revenue shall originate in the House of Representatives; but the Senate may propose or concur with Amendments as on other Bills.

Every Bill which shall have passed the House of Representatives and the Senate, shall, before it become a Law, be presented to the President of the United States; If he approves he shall sign it, but if not he shall return it, with his Objections to that House in which it shall have originated, who shall enter the Objections at large on their Journal, and proceed to reconsider it. If after such Reconsideration two thirds of that House shall agree to pass the Bill, it shall be sent, together with the Objections, to the other House, by which it shall likewise be reconsidered, and if approved by two thirds of that House, it shall become a Law. But in all such Cases the Votes of both Houses shall be determined by yeas and Nays, and the Names of the Persons voting for and against the Bill shall be entered on the Journal of each House respectively. If any Bill shall not be returned by the President within ten Days (Sundays excepted) after it shall have been presented to him, the Same shall be a Law, in like Manner as if he had signed it, unless the Congress by their Adjournment prevent its Return, in which Case it shall not be a Law.

Every Order, Resolution, or Vote to which the Concurrence of the Senate and House of Representatives may be necessary (except on a question of Adjournment) shall be presented to the President of the United States; and before the Same shall take Effect, shall be approved by him, or being disapproved by him, shall be repassed by two thirds of the Senate and House of Representatives, according to the Rules and Limitations prescribed in the Case of a Bill.

Section. 8.

The Congress shall have Power To lay and collect Taxes, Duties, Imposts and Excises, to pay the Debts and provide for the common Defense and general Welfare of the United States; but all Duties, Imposts and Excises shall be uniform throughout the United States;

To borrow Money on the credit of the United States;

To regulate Commerce with foreign Nations, and among the several States, and with the Indian Tribes;

To establish a uniform Rule of Naturalization, and uniform Laws on the subject of Bankruptcies throughout the United States;

To coin Money, regulate the Value thereof, and of foreign Coin, and fix the Standard of Weights and Measures;

To provide for the Punishment of counterfeiting the Securities and current Coin of the United States;

To establish Post Offices and post Roads;

To promote the Progress of Science and useful Arts, by securing for limited Times to Authors and Inventors the exclusive Right to their respective Writings and Discoveries;

To constitute Tribunals inferior to the supreme Court;

To define and punish Piracies and Felonies committed on the high Seas, and Offences against the Law of Nations;

To declare War, grant Letters of Marque and Reprisal, and make Rules concerning Captures on Land and Water;

To raise and support Armies, but no Appropriation of Money to that Use shall be for a longer Term than two Years;

To provide and maintain a Navy;

To make Rules for the Government and Regulation of the land and naval Forces;

To provide for calling forth the Militia to execute the Laws of the Union, suppress Insurrections and repel Invasions;

To provide for organizing, arming, and disciplining, the Militia, and for governing such Part of them as may be employed in the Service of the United States, reserving to the States respectively, the Appointment of the Officers, and the Authority of training the Militia according to the discipline prescribed by Congress;

To exercise exclusive Legislation in all Cases whatsoever, over such District (not exceeding ten Miles square) as may, by Cession of particular States, and the Acceptance of Congress, become the Seat of the Government of the United States, and to exercise like Authority over all Places purchased by the Consent of the Legislature of the State in which the Same shall be, for the Erection of Forts, Magazines, Arsenals, dock-Yards, and other needful Buildings; - And

To make all Laws which shall be necessary and proper for carrying into Execution the foregoing Powers, and all other Powers vested by this Constitution in the Government of the United States, or in any Department or Officer thereof.

Section. 9.

The Migration or Importation of such Persons as any of the States now existing shall think proper to admit, shall not be prohibited by the Congress prior to the Year one thousand eight hundred and eight, but a Tax or duty may be imposed on such Importation, not exceeding ten dollars for each Person.

The Privilege of the Writ of Habeas Corpus shall not be suspended, unless when in Cases of Rebellion or Invasion the public Safety may require it.

No Bill of Attainder or ex post facto Law shall be passed.

No Capitation, or other direct, Tax shall be laid, unless in Proportion to the Census or enumeration herein before directed to be taken.

No Tax or Duty shall be laid on Articles exported from any State.

No Preference shall be given by any Regulation of Commerce or Revenue to the Ports of one State over those of another: nor shall Vessels bound to, or from, one State, be obliged to enter, clear, or pay Duties in another.

No Money shall be drawn from the Treasury, but in Consequence of Appropriations made by Law; and a regular Statement and Account of the Receipts and Expenditures of all public Money shall be published from time to time.

No Title of Nobility shall be granted by the United States: And no Person holding any Office of Profit or Trust under them, shall, without the Consent of the Congress, accept of any present, Emolument, Office, or Title, of any kind whatever, from any King, Prince, or foreign State.

Section. 10.

No State shall enter into any Treaty, Alliance, or Confederation; grant Letters of Marque and Reprisal; coin Money; emit Bills of Credit; make any Thing but gold and silver Coin a Tender in Payment of Debts; pass any Bill of Attainder, ex post facto Law, or Law impairing the Obligation of Contracts, or grant any Title of Nobility.

No State shall, without the Consent of the Congress, lay any Imposts or Duties on Imports or Exports, except what may be absolutely necessary for executing it's inspection Laws: and the net Produce of all Duties and Imposts, laid by any State on Imports or Exports, shall be for the Use of the Treasury of the United States; and all such Laws shall be subject to the Revision and Control of the Congress.

No State shall, without the Consent of Congress, lay any Duty of Tonnage, keep Troops, or Ships of War in time of Peace, enter into any Agreement or Compact with another State, or with a foreign Power, or engage in War, unless actually invaded, or in such imminent Danger as will not admit of delay.

Article. II.

Section. 1.

The executive Power shall be vested in a President of the United States of America. He shall hold his Office during the Term of four Years, and, together with the

Vice President, chosen for the same Term, be elected, as follows

Each State shall appoint, in such Manner as the Legislature thereof may direct, a Number of Electors, equal to the whole Number of Senators and Representatives to which the State may be entitled in the Congress: but no Senator or Representative, or Person holding an Office of Trust or Profit under the United States, shall be appointed an Elector.

The Electors shall meet in their respective States, and vote by Ballot for two Persons, of whom one at least shall not be an Inhabitant of the same State with themselves. And they shall make a List of all the Persons voted for, and of the Number of Votes for each; which List they shall sign and certify, and transmit sealed to the Seat of the Government of the United States, directed to the President of the Senate. The President of the Senate shall, in the Presence of the Senate and House of Representatives, open all the Certificates, and the Votes shall then be counted. The Person having the greatest Number of Votes shall be the President, if such Number be a Majority of the whole Number of Electors appointed; and if there be more than one who have such Majority, and have an equal Number of Votes, then the House of Representatives shall immediately choose by Ballot one of them for President; and if no Person have a Majority, then from the five highest on the List the said House shall in like Manner choose the President. But in choosing the President, the Votes shall be taken by States, the Representation from each State having one Vote; A quorum for this Purpose shall consist of a

Member or Members from two thirds of the States, and a Majority of all the States shall be necessary to a Choice. In every Case, after the Choice of the President, the Person having the greatest Number of Votes of the Electors shall be the Vice President. But if there should remain two or more who have equal Votes, the Senate shall choose from them by Ballot the Vice President.

The Congress may determine the Time of choosing the Electors, and the Day on which they shall give their Votes; which Day shall be the same throughout the United States.

No Person except a natural born Citizen, or a Citizen of the United States, at the time of the Adoption of this Constitution, shall be eligible to the Office of President; neither shall any Person be eligible to that Office who shall not have attained to the Age of thirty-five Years, and been fourteen Years a Resident within the United States.

In Case of the Removal of the President from Office, or of his Death, Resignation, or Inability to discharge the Powers and Duties of the said Office, the Same shall devolve on the Vice President, and the Congress may by Law provide for the Case of Removal, Death, Resignation or Inability, both of the President and Vice President, declaring what Officer shall then act as President, and such Officer shall act accordingly, until the Disability be removed, or a President shall be elected.

The President shall, at stated Times, receive for his Services, a Compensation, which shall neither be increased nor diminished during the Period for which he shall have been elected, and he shall not receive within that Period any other Emolument from the United States, or any of them.

Before he enter on the Execution of his Office, he shall take the following Oath or Affirmation: - "I do solemnly swear (or affirm) that I will faithfully execute the Office of President of the United States, and will to the best of my Ability, preserve, protect and defend the Constitution of the United States."

Section. 2.

The President shall be Commander in Chief of the Army and Navy of the United States, and of the Militia of the several States, when called into the actual Service of the United States; he may require the Opinion, in writing, of the principal Officer in each of the executive Departments, upon any Subject relating to the Duties of their respective Offices, and he shall have Power to grant Reprieves and Pardons for Offences against the United States, except in Cases of Impeachment.

He shall have Power, by and with the Advice and Consent of the Senate, to make Treaties, provided two thirds of the Senators present concur; and he shall nominate, and by and with the Advice and Consent of the Senate, shall appoint Ambassadors, other public Ministers and Consuls, Judges of the supreme Court, and all other Officers of the United States, whose Appointments are not herein otherwise provided for, and which shall be established by Law: but the

Congress may by Law vest the Appointment of such inferior Officers, as they think proper, in the President alone, in the Courts of Law, or in the Heads of Departments.

The President shall have Power to fill up all Vacancies that may happen during the Recess of the Senate, by granting Commissions which shall expire at the End of their next Session.

Section. 3.

He shall from time to time give to the Congress Information of the State of the Union, and recommend to their Consideration such Measures as he shall judge necessary and expedient; he may, on extraordinary Occasions, convene both Houses, or either of them, and in Case of Disagreement between them, with Respect to the Time of Adjournment, he may adjourn them to such Time as he shall think proper; he shall receive Ambassadors and other public Ministers; he shall take Care that the Laws be faithfully executed, and shall Commission all the Officers of the United States.

Section. 4.

The President, Vice President and all civil Officers of the United States, shall be removed from Office on Impeachment for, and Conviction of, Treason, Bribery, or other high Crimes and Misdemeanors.

Article III.

Section. 1.

The judicial Power of the United States, shall be vested in one supreme Court, and in such inferior Courts as the Congress may from time to time ordain and establish. The Judges, both of the supreme and inferior Courts, shall hold their Offices during good Behaviour, and shall, at stated Times, receive for their Services, a Compensation, which shall not be diminished during their Continuance in Office.

Section. 2.

The judicial Power shall extend to all Cases, in Law and Equity, arising under this Constitution, the Laws of the United States, and Treaties made, or which shall be made, under their Authority;—to all Cases affecting Ambassadors, other public Ministers and Consuls;—to all Cases of admiralty and maritime Jurisdiction;—to Controversies to which the United States shall be a Party;—to Controversies between two or more States;— between a State and Citizens of another State,—between Citizens of different States,—between Citizens of the same State claiming Lands under Grants of different States, and between a State, or the Citizens thereof, and foreign States, Citizens or Subjects.

In all Cases affecting Ambassadors, other public Ministers and Consuls, and those in which a State shall be Party, the supreme Court shall have original Jurisdiction. In all the other Cases before mentioned, the supreme Court shall have appellate Jurisdiction, both as to Law and Fact, with such Exceptions, and under such Regulations as the Congress shall make.

The Trial of all Crimes, except in Cases of Impeachment, shall be by Jury; and such Trial shall be held in the State where the said Crimes shall have been committed; but when not committed within any State, the Trial shall be at such Place or Places as the Congress may by Law have directed.

Section. 3.

Treason against the United States, shall consist only in levying War against them, or in adhering to their Enemies, giving them Aid and Comfort. No Person shall be convicted of Treason unless on the Testimony of two Witnesses to the same overt Act, or on Confession in open Court.

The Congress shall have Power to declare the Punishment of Treason, but no Attainder of Treason shall work Corruption of Blood, or Forfeiture except during the Life of the Person attainted.

Article. IV.

Section. 1.

Full Faith and Credit shall be given in each State to the public Acts, Records, and judicial Proceedings of every other State. And the Congress may by general Laws prescribe the Manner in which such Acts,

Records and Proceedings shall be proved, and the Effect thereof.

Section. 2.

The Citizens of each State shall be entitled to all Privileges and Immunities of Citizens in the several States.

A Person charged in any State with Treason, Felony, or other Crime, who shall flee from Justice, and be found in another State, shall on Demand of the executive Authority of the State from which he fled, be delivered up, to be removed to the State having Jurisdiction of the Crime.

No Person held to Service or Labour in one State, under the Laws thereof, escaping into another, shall, in Consequence of any Law or Regulation therein, be discharged from such Service or Labour, but shall be delivered up on Claim of the Party to whom such Service or Labour may be due.

Section. 3.

New States may be admitted by the Congress into this Union; but no new State shall be formed or erected within the Jurisdiction of any other State; nor any State be formed by the Junction of two or more States, or Parts of States, without the Consent of the Legislatures of the States concerned as well as of the Congress.

The Congress shall have Power to dispose of and make all needful Rules and Regulations respecting the Territory or other Property belonging to the United

States; and nothing in this Constitution shall be so construed as to Prejudice any Claims of the United States, or of any particular State.

Section. 4.

The United States shall guarantee to every State in this Union a Republican Form of Government, and shall protect each of them against Invasion; and on Application of the Legislature, or of the Executive (when the Legislature cannot be convened), against domestic Violence.

Article. V.

The Congress, whenever two thirds of both Houses shall deem it necessary, shall propose Amendments to this Constitution, or, on the Application of the Legislatures of two thirds of the several States, shall call a Convention for proposing Amendments, which, in either Case, shall be valid to all Intents and Purposes, as Part of this Constitution, when ratified by the Legislatures of three fourths of the several States, or by Conventions in three fourths thereof, as the one or the other Mode of Ratification may be proposed by the Congress; Provided that no Amendment which may be made prior to the Year One thousand eight hundred and eight shall in any Manner affect the first and fourth Clauses in the Ninth Section of the first Article; and that no State, without its Consent, shall be deprived of its equal Suffrage in the Senate.

Article. VI.

All Debts contracted and Engagements entered into, before the Adoption of this Constitution, shall be as valid against the United States under this Constitution, as under the Confederation.

This Constitution, and the Laws of the United States which shall be made in Pursuance thereof; and all Treaties made, or which shall be made, under the Authority of the United States, shall be the supreme Law of the Land; and the Judges in every State shall be bound thereby, any Thing in the Constitution or Laws of any State to the Contrary notwithstanding.

The Senators and Representatives before mentioned, and the Members of the several State Legislatures, and all executive and judicial Officers, both of the United States and of the several States, shall be bound by Oath or Affirmation, to support this Constitution; but no religious Test shall ever be required as a Qualification to any Office or public Trust under the United States.

Article. VII.

The Ratification of the Conventions of nine States, shall be sufficient for the Establishment of this Constitution between the States so ratifying the Same.

The U.S. Bill of Rights

The Preamble to The Bill of Rights

Congress of the United States
begun and held at the City of New-York, on
Wednesday the fourth of March, one thousand
seven hundred and eighty-nine.

THE Conventions of a number of the States, having at the time of their adopting the Constitution, expressed a desire, in order to prevent misconstruction or abuse of its powers, that further declaratory and restrictive clauses should be added: And as extending the ground of public confidence in the Government, will best ensure the beneficent ends of its institution.

RESOLVED by the Senate and House of Representatives of the United States of America, in Congress assembled, two thirds of both Houses concurring, that the following Articles be proposed to the Legislatures of the several States, as amendments to the Constitution of the United States, all, or any of which Articles, when ratified by three fourths of the said Legislatures, to be valid to all intents and purposes, as part of the said Constitution; viz.

ARTICLES in addition to, and Amendment of the Constitution of the United States of America, proposed by Congress, and ratified by the Legislatures of the several States, pursuant to the fifth Article of the original Constitution.

Note: The following text is a transcription of the first ten amendments to the Constitution in their original form. These amendments were ratified December 15, 1791, and form what is known as the "Bill of Rights."

Amendment I

Congress shall make no law respecting an establishment of religion, or prohibiting the free exercise thereof; or abridging the freedom of speech, or of the press; or the right of the people peaceably to assemble, and to petition the Government for a redress of grievances.

Amendment II

A well-regulated Militia, being necessary to the security of a free State, the right of the people to keep and bear Arms, shall not be infringed.

Amendment III

No Soldier shall, in time of peace be quartered in any house, without the consent of the Owner, nor in time of war, but in a manner to be prescribed by law.

Amendment IV

The right of the people to be secure in their persons, houses, papers, and effects, against unreasonable searches and seizures, shall not be violated, and no Warrants shall issue, but upon probable cause, supported by Oath or affirmation, and particularly describing the place to be searched, and the persons or things to be seized.

Amendment V

No person shall be held to answer for a capital, or
otherwise infamous crime, unless on a presentment or
indictment of a Grand Jury, except in cases arising in
the land or naval forces, or in the Militia, when in
actual service in time of War or public danger; nor
shall any person be subject for the same offence to be
twice put in jeopardy of life or limb; nor shall be
compelled in any criminal case to be a witness against
himself, nor be deprived of life, liberty, or property,
without due process of law; nor shall private property
be taken for public use, without just compensation.

Amendment VI

In all criminal prosecutions, the accused shall enjoy
the right to a speedy and public trial, by an impartial
jury of the State and district wherein the crime shall
have been committed, which district shall have been
previously ascertained by law, and to be informed of
the nature and cause of the accusation; to be
confronted with the witnesses against him; to have
compulsory process for obtaining witnesses in his
favor, and to have the Assistance of Counsel for his
defense.

Amendment VII

In Suits at common law, where the value in
controversy shall exceed twenty dollars, the right of
trial by jury shall be preserved, and no fact tried by a
jury, shall be otherwise re-examined in any Court of

the United States, than according to the rules of the common law.

Amendment VIII

Excessive bail shall not be required, nor excessive fines imposed, nor cruel and unusual punishments inflicted.

Amendment IX

The enumeration in the Constitution, of certain rights, shall not be construed to deny or disparage others retained by the people.

Amendment X

The powers not delegated to the United States by the Constitution, nor prohibited by it to the States, are reserved to the States respectively, or to the people.

Additional Amendments to the U. S. Constitution

Amendment XI

Passed by Congress March 4, 1794. Ratified February 7, 1795. Note: Article III, section 2, of the Constitution was modified by amendment 11.

The Judicial power of the United States shall not be construed to extend to any suit in law or equity, commenced or prosecuted against one of the United

States by Citizens of another State, or by Citizens or Subjects of any Foreign State.

Amendment XII

Passed by Congress December 9, 1803. Ratified June 15, 1804. Note: A portion of Article II, section 1 of the Constitution was superseded by the 12th amendment.

The Electors shall meet in their respective states and vote by ballot for President and Vice-President, one of whom, at least, shall not be an inhabitant of the same state with themselves; they shall name in their ballots the person voted for as President, and in distinct ballots the person voted for as Vice-President, and they shall make distinct lists of all persons voted for as President, and of all persons voted for as Vice-President, and of the number of votes for each, which lists they shall sign and certify, and transmit sealed to the seat of the government of the United States, directed to the President of the Senate; -- the President of the Senate shall, in the presence of the Senate and House of Representatives, open all the certificates and the votes shall then be counted; -- The person having the greatest number of votes for President, shall be the President, if such number be a majority of the whole number of Electors appointed; and if no person have such majority, then from the persons having the highest numbers not exceeding three on the list of those voted for as President, the House of Representatives shall choose immediately, by ballot, the President. But in choosing the President, the votes shall be taken by states, the representation from each state having one vote; a quorum for this purpose shall

consist of a member or members from two-thirds of the states, and a majority of all the states shall be necessary to a choice. [And if the House of Representatives shall not choose a President whenever the right of choice shall devolve upon them, before the fourth day of March next following, then the Vice-President shall act as President, as in case of the death or other constitutional disability of the President.* The person having the greatest number of votes as Vice-President, shall be the Vice-President, if such number be a majority of the whole number of Electors appointed, and if no person have a majority, then from the two highest numbers on the list, the Senate shall choose the Vice-President; a quorum for the purpose shall consist of two-thirds of the whole number of Senators, and a majority of the whole number shall be necessary to a choice. But no person constitutionally incligible to the office of President shall be eligible to that of Vice-President of the United States.
*Superseded by section 3 of the 20th amendment.

Amendment XIII

Passed by Congress January 31, 1865. Ratified December 6, 1865. Note: A portion of Article IV, section 2, of the Constitution was superseded by the 13th amendment.

Section 1.
Neither slavery nor involuntary servitude, except as a punishment for crime whereof the party shall have been duly convicted, shall exist within the United States, or any place subject to their jurisdiction.

Section 2.
Congress shall have power to enforce this article by
appropriate legislation.

Amendment XIV

*Passed by Congress June 13, 1866. Ratified July 9,
1868. Note: Article I, section 2, of the Constitution was
modified by section 2 of the 14th amendment.*

Section 1.
All persons born or naturalized in the United States,
and subject to the jurisdiction thereof, are citizens of
the United States and of the State wherein they reside.
No State shall make or enforce any law which shall
abridge the privileges or immunities of citizens of the
United States; nor shall any State deprive any person
of life, liberty, or property, without due process of law;
nor deny to any person within its jurisdiction the equal
protection of the laws.

Section 2.
Representatives shall be apportioned among the
several States according to their respective numbers,
counting the whole number of persons in each State,
excluding Indians not taxed. But when the right to vote
at any election for the choice of electors for President
and Vice-President of the United States,
Representatives in Congress, the Executive and
Judicial officers of a State, or the members of the
Legislature thereof, is denied to any of the male
inhabitants of such State, being twenty-one years of
age,* and citizens of the United States, or in any way
abridged, except for participation in rebellion, or other

crime, the basis of representation therein shall be reduced in the proportion which the number of such male citizens shall bear to the whole number of male citizens twenty-one years of age in such State.

Section 3.
No person shall be a Senator or Representative in Congress, or elector of President and Vice-President, or hold any office, civil or military, under the United States, or under any State, who, having previously taken an oath, as a member of Congress, or as an officer of the United States, or as a member of any State legislature, or as an executive or judicial officer of any State, to support the Constitution of the United States, shall have engaged in insurrection or rebellion against the same, or given aid or comfort to the enemies thereof. But Congress may by a vote of two-thirds of each House, remove such disability.

Section 4.
The validity of the public debt of the United States, authorized by law, including debts incurred for payment of pensions and bounties for services in suppressing insurrection or rebellion, shall not be questioned. But neither the United States nor any State shall assume or pay any debt or obligation incurred in aid of insurrection or rebellion against the United States, or any claim for the loss or emancipation of any slave; but all such debts, obligations and claims shall be held illegal and void.

Section 5.
The Congress shall have the power to enforce, by

appropriate legislation, the provisions of this article.
*Changed by section 1 of the 26th amendment.

Amendment XV

Passed by Congress February 26, 1869. Ratified February 3, 1870.

Section 1.
The right of citizens of the United States to vote shall not be denied or abridged by the United States or by any State on account of race, color, or previous condition of servitude--

Section 2.
The Congress shall have the power to enforce this article by appropriate legislation.

Amendment XVI

Passed by Congress July 2, 1909. Ratified February 3, 1913. Note: Article I, section 9, of the Constitution was modified by amendment 16.

The Congress shall have power to lay and collect taxes on incomes, from whatever source derived, without apportionment among the several States, and without regard to any census or enumeration.

Amendment XVII

Passed by Congress May 13, 1912. Ratified April 8, 1913. Note: Article I, section 3, of the Constitution was modified by the 17th amendment.

The Senate of the United States shall be composed of two Senators from each State, elected by the people thereof, for six years; and each Senator shall have one vote. The electors in each State shall have the qualifications requisite for electors of the most numerous branch of the State legislatures.

When vacancies happen in the representation of any State in the Senate, the executive authority of such State shall issue writs of election to fill such vacancies: Provided, That the legislature of any State may empower the executive thereof to make temporary appointments until the people fill the vacancies by election as the legislature may direct.

This amendment shall not be so construed as to affect the election or term of any Senator chosen before it becomes valid as part of the Constitution.

Amendment XVIII

Passed by Congress December 18, 1917. Ratified January 16, 1919. Repealed by amendment 21.

Section 1.
After one year from the ratification of this article the manufacture, sale, or transportation of intoxicating liquors within, the importation thereof into, or the exportation thereof from the United States and all territory subject to the jurisdiction thereof for beverage purposes is hereby prohibited.

Section 2.
The Congress and the several States shall have

concurrent power to enforce this article by appropriate legislation.

Section 3.
This article shall be inoperative unless it shall have been ratified as an amendment to the Constitution by the legislatures of the several States, as provided in the Constitution, within seven years from the date of the submission hereof to the States by the Congress.

Amendment XIX

Passed by Congress June 4, 1919. Ratified August 18, 1920.

The right of citizens of the United States to vote shall not be denied or abridged by the United States or by any State on account of sex. Congress shall have power to enforce this article by appropriate legislation.

Amendment XX

Passed by Congress March 2, 1932. Ratified January 23, 1933. Note: Article I, section 4, of the Constitution was modified by section 2 of this amendment. In addition, a portion of the 12th amendment was superseded by section 3.

Section 1.
The terms of the President and the Vice President shall end at noon on the 20th day of January, and the terms of Senators and Representatives at noon on the 3d day of January, of the years in which such terms would have ended if this article had not been ratified; and the terms of their successors shall then begin.

Section 2.
The Congress shall assemble at least once in every
year, and such meeting shall begin at noon on the 3d
day of January, unless they shall by law appoint a
different day.

Section 3.
If, at the time fixed for the beginning of the term of the
President, the President elect shall have died, the Vice
President elect shall become President. If a President
shall not have been chosen before the time fixed for
the beginning of his term, or if the President elect shall
have failed to qualify, then the Vice President elect
shall act as President until a President shall have
qualified; and the Congress may by law provide for the
case wherein neither a President elect nor a Vice
President shall have qualified, declaring who shall then
act as President, or the manner in which one who is to
act shall be selected, and such person shall act
accordingly until a President or Vice President shall
have qualified.

Section 4.
The Congress may by law provide for the case of the
death of any of the persons from whom the House of
Representatives may choose a President whenever the
right of choice shall have devolved upon them, and for
the case of the death of any of the persons from whom
the Senate may choose a Vice President whenever the
right of choice shall have devolved upon them.

Section 5.
Sections 1 and 2 shall take effect on the 15th day of
October following the ratification of this article.

Section 6.
This article shall be inoperative unless it shall have been ratified as an amendment to the Constitution by the legislatures of three-fourths of the several States within seven years from the date of its submission.

Amendment XXI

Passed by Congress February 20, 1933. Ratified December 5, 1933.

Section 1.
The eighteenth article of amendment to the Constitution of the United States is hereby repealed.

Section 2.
The transportation or importation into any State, Territory, or Possession of the United States for delivery or use therein of intoxicating liquors, in violation of the laws thereof, is hereby prohibited.

Section 3.
This article shall be inoperative unless it shall have been ratified as an amendment to the Constitution by conventions in the several States, as provided in the Constitution, within seven years from the date of the submission hereof to the States by the Congress.

Amendment XXII

Passed by Congress March 21, 1947. Ratified February 27, 1951.

Section 1.
No person shall be elected to the office of the

President more than twice, and no person who has held the office of President, or acted as President, for more than two years of a term to which some other person was elected President shall be elected to the office of President more than once. But this Article shall not apply to any person holding the office of President when this Article was proposed by Congress, and shall not prevent any person who may be holding the office of President, or acting as President, during the term within which this Article becomes operative from holding the office of President or acting as President during the remainder of such term.

Section 2.
This article shall be inoperative unless it shall have been ratified as an amendment to the Constitution by the legislatures of three-fourths of the several States within seven years from the date of its submission to the States by the Congress.

Amendment XXIII

Passed by Congress June 16, 1960. Ratified March 29, 1961.

Section 1.
The District constituting the seat of Government of the United States shall appoint in such manner as Congress may direct: A number of electors of President and Vice President equal to the whole number of Senators and Representatives in Congress to which the District would be entitled if it were a State, but in no event more than the least populous State; they shall be in addition to those appointed by the

States, but they shall be considered, for the purposes of the election of President and Vice President, to be electors appointed by a State; and they shall meet in the District and perform such duties as provided by the twelfth article of amendment.

Section 2.
The Congress shall have power to enforce this article by appropriate legislation.

Amendment XXIV

Passed by Congress August 27, 1962. Ratified January 23, 1964.

Section 1.
The right of citizens of the United States to vote in any primary or other election for President or Vice President, for electors for President or Vice President, or for Senator or Representative in Congress, shall not be denied or abridged by the United States or any State by reason of failure to pay poll tax or other tax.

Section 2.
The Congress shall have power to enforce this article by appropriate legislation.

Amendment XXV

Passed by Congress July 6, 1965. Ratified February 10, 1967. Note: Article II, section 1, of the Constitution was affected by the 25th amendment.

Section 1.
In case of the removal of the President from office or

of his death or resignation, the Vice President shall become President.

Section 2.
Whenever there is a vacancy in the office of the Vice President, the President shall nominate a Vice President who shall take office upon confirmation by a majority vote of both Houses of Congress.

Section 3.
Whenever the President transmits to the President pro tempore of the Senate and the Speaker of the House of Representatives his written declaration that he is unable to discharge the powers and duties of his office, and until he transmits to them a written declaration to the contrary, such powers and duties shall be discharged by the Vice President as Acting President.

Section 4.
Whenever the Vice President and a majority of either the principal officers of the executive departments or of such other body as Congress may by law provide, transmit to the President pro tempore of the Senate and the Speaker of the House of Representatives their written declaration that the President is unable to discharge the powers and duties of his office, the Vice President shall immediately assume the powers and duties of the office as Acting President.

Thereafter, when the President transmits to the President pro tempore of the Senate and the Speaker of the House of Representatives his written declaration that no inability exists, he shall resume the powers and duties of his office unless the Vice President and a majority of either the principal officers of the executive department or of such other body as Congress may by law provide, transmit within four days to the President pro tempore of the Senate and the Speaker of the House of Representatives their written declaration that the President is unable to discharge the powers and duties of his office.

Thereupon Congress shall decide the issue, assembling within forty-eight hours for that purpose if not in session. If the Congress, within twenty-one days after receipt of the latter written declaration, or, if Congress is not in session, within twenty-one days after Congress is required to assemble, determines by two-thirds vote of both Houses that the President is unable to discharge the powers and duties of his office, the Vice President shall continue to discharge the same as Acting President; otherwise, the President shall resume the powers and duties of his office.

Amendment XXVI

Passed by Congress March 23, 1971. Ratified July 1, 1971. Note: Amendment 14, section 2, of the Constitution was modified by section 1 of the 26th amendment.

Section 1.
The right of citizens of the United States, who are eighteen years of age or older, to vote shall not be denied or abridged by the United States or by any State on account of age.

Section 2.
The Congress shall have power to enforce this article by appropriate legislation.

Amendment XXVII

Originally proposed Sept. 25, 1789. Ratified May 7, 1992.

No law, varying the compensation for the services of the Senators and Representatives, shall take effect, until an election of representatives shall have intervened.

Media Law & Ethics

Dr. George Padgett
Office: 208A Schar (The Produce Pod)
Cell: 336-214-0540 / e-mail: padgettg@elon.edu

Note: The following is a sample based on the Spring 2017 syllabus used by the author at Elon University. Current students will receive an updated syllabus with a schedule of classes and individual assignments on the class Moodle site.

Description: The First Amendment is the philosophical foundation for freedom of speech and press in America. This course distinguishes between forms of communication that have constitutional protection and those with limitations (libel, privacy, copyright, censorship, commercial speech, broadcast licensing, access to information). Students explore the foundations of moral reasoning and apply ethical responsibilities to communications cases.

Goal: This course will examine the legal foundations for freedom of speech and the press and familiarize students with legal restrictions and ethical principles relevant to media practitioners.

Objectives: Upon completion of this course, students will be able to:

1. Identify the five freedoms outlined in the First Amendment and state their importance in a democracy.

2. Distinguish between areas of "speech and press" that are and are not protectedby the First Amendment.

3. Apply major legal principles associated with freedom of expression, such as libel, privacy, copyright and government regulations.

4. Describe the role of professional ethics codes and their relationship to ethical ways of reasoning and decision-making.

5. Identify and analyze ethical issues involved in case studies and explain the philosophical and professional considerations that underpin the analysis.

6. Apply ethical principles to contemporary issues and to one's own practice of a professional discipline

Professional Standards: The School of Communications' Professional Standards Policy statement is posted on our class Moodle site. Please read and become familiar with all school policies.

Attendance: Absences beyond the equivalent of one week will result in lowering the final grade by one-third of a letter grade for each absence.

Assignments: Except in the case of excused absences, assignments will not be accepted after their due date. All assignments must be submitted in class (not by email). Work missed due to an excused absence must be made up within one period of your return to class.

Late Arrivals: Attendance is taken only at the beginning of class. If you are late, it is your responsibility to see me after class. Two occasions of excessive tardiness will be counted as an absence.

On Doing Your Own Work: You are responsible for doing your own work. Failure to do so in any instance will result in a failing grade in the class.

Students with Disabilities: If you are a student with a documented disability who will require accommodations in this course, please register with Disabilities Services in the Duke Building, Room 108 (278-6500), for assistance in developing a plan to address your academic needs.

Religious Holidays Policies: In supporting religious diversity, Elon has a policy and procedures for students who wish to observe religious holidays. Students who wish to observe a holiday during the semester must complete the online Religious Observance Notification Form (RONF), available at the following website within the first two weeks of the semester. *http://www.elon.edu/eweb/students/religiou s_life/ Religious Holidays.xhtml* This policy does not apply during the final examination period. Students are required to make prior arrangements with the instructor for completion of any work missed during the absence. Students may contact the Truitt Center staff with any questions (336-278-7729).

Grading: Course content is graded as follows and grading will be based on a system of 500 points:

100 points - Exams 1-3 (each)
125 points - Comprehensive Final Exam
50 points - Miscellaneous (Case studies, hypotheticals, current topics etc.)
25 points - Research Project

Grading Scale: Points reflect the normal percentage scale: 93%> = A; 90-92% = A-; 87-89% = B+; 83-86% = B; 80-82% = B- etc.

Resources: There is no required textbook for this course. Reading assignments as listed on the syllabus can be linked directly from the electronic version of the syllabus posted on Moodle. Study materials are also available. If you would prefer an actual textbook, course content follows *Communications Law*, John Zelezny, Thomson Wadsworth. It is available for rent or electronically at http://www.cengage.com

Search "Zelezny" in the Higher Education Catalog. You also could purchase a recent edition version of the text on Amazon for minimal cost.

Miscellaneous: The following assignments will be due throughout the semester as indicated on the attached schedule. Each of you will do a case report and a current topics presentation.

1. Case Reports: Each student will present one specific case report to the class and turn in a typed 2-3 page summary of the case with the written reports to be divided into the following sections: Introduction (facts of the case), Arguments (plaintiff and defendant), Decision of the court (summarizing and quoting from significant parts of the decision), and Significance (why case is important). Case reports are due on the day of presentation. Late is not an option. Cite sources.

2. Current Topics: Written accounts of recent or current/ongoing legal or ethical issues/situations from newspaper, magazine, or online research. Papers should include five summaries of recent cases/situations. Due dates are indicated on the schedule of classes. Where possible link the current issues to cases studied in class. Cite all sources.

3. Hypotheticals: Written analysis of hypothetical legal situations. You will be given a situation at the end of a class period and have until the next class to research the hypothetical and write a one-page response predicting how the legal system would respond, citing and explaining actual case precedents. Cite all sources.

4. Transparency Project: Research and analysis of the controversies created by activists Daniel Ellsberg, Julian Assange, Chelsea Manning, and Edward Snowden.

5. Special Assignments: Additional brief assignments related to ongoing news and/or court decisions will likely be given and will be figured into the miscellaneous portion of your grade.

Research: Research projects on media law or ethics topics will be completed by teams of two or three people, the teams to be selected randomly by the instructor. Presentations must relate directly to media law and/or ethics and should not be repetitious of material covered in class. And, YES, content from the presentations will be on the final exam. In fact, 5 - 10 questions on the exam will be from the research presentations.

Presentation Requirements:

1. Presentations must be thoroughly researched using a variety of sources including personal interviews, academic/professional journals, books, newspapers, magazines, and documented Internet sources
2. Presentations should be approximately 30 minutes in length. Allow time for discussion.
3. When researching your topic, think depth rather than breadth.
4. Team members must participate AND should work together to create an effective, coherent presentation. Not two or three separate presentations.
5. Each team should turn in an outline of the research, a bibliography, a printed copy of the PowerPoint presentation and a brief "study guide" of major points (copied for distribution to the class).

6. Videos, illustrations & handouts should be used where appropriate to illustrate points.
7. Use PowerPoint for illustrations, links, bullet points.
8. Do not read your presentation!
9. All sources must be cited.

Possible Research Topics Include the following:

1. Hate & Homophobia in the Open Marketplace. Snyder v. Phelps and the Westboro Baptist Church. Could also talk about Pastor Terry Jones and his crusade against Islam.

2. Violence and Free Expression in Video Games: Schwarzenegger/Brown v. Video Software Dealers Association. Presentation should include examples of contemporary video games.

3. Social Media and Privacy Issues (Facebook, Twitter, YouTube, FourSquare etc.) Discuss social media privacy policies and recent cases/controversies.

4. New technology and privacy issues: cell phone cameras, phone gps and tracking devices, drones, Google glasses and other wearable electronics etc. Look specifically at U.S. v. Jones, a recent case involving warrantless use of a tracking device to follow the movements of private citizens.

5. Copyright and downloading of music, movies etc. We've talked about the Napster and Grokster cases, so don't dwell on those. Find out what's going on now in this continuing struggle between consumers and copyright holders. Include discussion of Creative Commons.

6. Ethical and Legal issues related to reality TV (include liability issues). In addition to profiling reality TV as it exists today, look at some specific programs and how they handle legal (privacy) and ethical issues related to participants. Are they putting participants in danger? Are they legally responsible? Should there be industry standards?

7. Cyber bullying and First Amendment Implications. Identify important/controversial cases/situations related to cyber bullying. Look at state and federal laws that have been passed to address concerns. Are these laws infringing on free speech rights?

8. First Amendment Across Cultures: Contrast American First Amendment with freedom of expression laws in other countries. Pick four or five countries that represent the range: Finland to North Korea etc. Reporters Without Border is a good reference.

9. Free speech in art (including photography). Where are the lines between artistic expression and obscenity/indecency? Classic cases past and current.

10. Violence and obscenity in cinema past and present. Include discussion of, censoring boards, the Hays Code, Burstyn v. Wilson and other cases.

11. Music and the First Amendment. Artists the likes of Eminem (rap/hip hop) and Madonna (female pop) have played a significant role in pushing the boundaries of free speech in music. Their groundbreaking work has provided broader rights for all of us.

12. In an era of post-truth, is the marketplace of ideas dead? Explain the origins of the marketplace, role in contemporary society and future given the divisiveness in politics and even in society in general. Also, consider its role, if any, in the future.

13. Other?? If you're interested in a topic that's not here, write a brief proposal, get it to me and I will consider adding it to the list.

Media Law/Ethics Related Websites

American Civil Liberties
Union: http://www.aclu.org

American Society of Newspaper
Editors: http://asne.org

Center for Journalism Ethics (case studies):
https://ethics.journalism.wisc.edu

Committee of Concerned
Journalists: http://www.concernedjournalists.org

Creative
Commons: http://www.creativecommons.org

Electronic Frontier
Foundation: http://www.eff.org

Electronic Privacy Information
Center: http://www.epic.org

Ethical Case Studies:
http://mediaschool.indiana.edu

Ethics Cases Studies/Society of Professional
Journalists: http://spj.org/ethicscasestudies

Federal Communications
Commission: http://www.fcc.gov

FindLaw – A professional site for accessing full-length legal cases and
summaries: http://www.findlaw.com

First Amendment Center:
http://www.firstamendmentcenter.org

Justia – a legal help site for finding everything
from lawyers to law schools: htp://www.justia.com

Motion Picture Association of
America: http://www.mpaa.org

National Association of
Broadcasters: http://www.nab.org

Oyez – a favorite case site for searching for full-length legal cases and
summaries: http://www.oyez.org

Public Relations Society of
America: http://www.prsa.org

Public Relations Student Society of America:
http://prssa.prsa.org

Radio Television Digital News
Association: http://www.rtnda.org

Society for Cinema and Media
Studies: http://www.cmstudies.org

Society of Professional
Journalists: http://www.spj.org

iMediaEthics (formerly stinkyjournalism.com): http://www.imediaethics.org

Student Press Law Center: http://www.splc.org

Supreme Court of the United States Blog: http://www.scotusblog.com

U.S. Supreme Court: http://www.supremecourt.gov

Made in the USA
Columbia, SC
02 March 2020